RESTORING PERIOD TIMBER-FRAMED HOUSES

RESTORING PERIOD TIMBER-FRAMED HOUSES

DAVID J. SWINDELLS

DAVID & CHARLES
Newton Abbot   London   North Pomfret (Vt)

To my wife Diana and
children Sebastian and Kate

British Library Cataloguing in Publication Data

Swindells, David J.
   Restoring period timber-framed houses.
   1. Wooden-frame houses – Conservation and
   restoration
   I. Title
   728.3′028′8   NA7173

   ISBN 0-7153-8526-7

Phototypeset by Typesetters (Birmingham) Ltd,
Smethwick, West Midlands
and printed in Great Britain
by Butler & Tanner Ltd, Frome
for David & Charles Publishers plc
Brunel House   Newton Abbot   Devon

Published in the United States of America
by David & Charles Inc
North Pomfret   Vermont 05053   USA

CONTENTS

ACKNOWLEDGEMENTS

I should like to acknowledge the help of the founder, director and staff of the Weald and Downland Open Air Museum at Singleton, West Sussex, for allowing me to photograph and sketch constructional details from buildings on display, and for supplying me with valuable record photographs of the erection of a timber frame.

FOREWORD

As a building surveyor I have the enviable, and sometimes not so enviable, task of crawling over other people's houses, largely with the view in mind of finding fault in order that my client may obtain a better bargain or at the very least a better idea and understanding of what he is letting himself in for if and when he buys the house in question.

In my fifteen years or so of practice experience, I have looked at some astonishing properties, and I can say that I am most in my element when clambering about in what must be one of the least understood, yet most loved and cherished pieces of English history, the period timber-framed house. When a survey is carried out on a timber-framed house, the object is to assess the state of the structure and to report its condition to the client. In doing this the surveyor is tightly bound by the ethics of his professional associations, and there is always the watchful eye of the professional indemnity insurance company and the absolute need to include standard legal phrases and exclusion clauses in the written report. The good surveyor will work through these restrictions and still convey his appreciation of the building and his enthusiasm for it, assuming that he has any, to his client who, captivated by the romantic vision of owning his ideal house, may or may not fully appreciate everything that he is proposing to take on.

A good surveyor will report fully on all defects found, including dampness, woodworm and fungal attack. Most people are reasonably familiar with these more common defects, but few will understand the many other defects which can occur as a result of, for instance, dampness. An apparently innocent garden level may cause a water penetration problem which has affected internal finishes, subfloor voids and structural timbers. The electrical wiring may be affected, as may other hidden services or parts of the essential structure which might not be readily apparent or of any great significance to the layman. The surveyor may also talk about the roofs and the way in which the hand-made clay-peg tiles are fixed. He will discuss the type and may offer some useful advice on maintenance. He will certainly discuss the external walls and may talk about corner posts, wind braces, bressummers and other mysterious structural elements. The client may well be interested in the structural analysis of the building, but he is likely to be disappointed that its history is not discussed in more detail or that more attention is not paid to his wife's prime concern as to whether the Welsh dresser will fit in the kitchen or the pine wardrobe in the bedroom, if indeed it is practically possible to get it up the oak staircase which seems inordinately narrow and steep and not at all what one is used to.

As a surveyor I have experienced confrontation with a prospective purchaser on a number of occasions and have explained and hopefully justified my comments accordingly. To add interest, I have attached a potted history of the building to the survey report covering items such as initial construction dates, later extensions, when a new staircase was added or the fireplace altered. Many aspects of the building's development can be foretold by visible evidence. Other less obvious aspects require a degree of interpretation, and it is largely because of this that I felt there was a need for a book – not a history of timber-framed buildings but an appraisal of details common in periods during the development process. Such a record of details and restoration techniques could be an aid to the owner or would-be purchaser in the understanding of exactly what he is committing himself to. The period timber-framed house is very different from the modern speculative 'box', and it is my experience that a majority of people move from the latter to the former. You hardly ever hear of people moving from the former to the latter. In addition to an understanding of the structural frame, it is my experience that owners are often interested in preserving and restoring the elements which go to form the roofs, walls and other parts of the building. Although many books are available on building construction and DIY, there are few on preservation and restoration techniques for period timber-framed houses.

This book is not intended to put surveyors and architects out of business, but more to enhance the relationship between an interested owner and his professional advisers. If it helps in some small way to preserve our building heritage, the effort that has gone into it will have been well worthwhile.

1 THE EARLY TIMBER FRAME

The early Saxon house was an exercise in elementary building technique using circular and rectangular plans. The external walls were often very low and frequently built partly below ground, the superstructure being a frame of two poles set in each corner and rising to meet in the centre, where a pole was affixed. This method of construction had been used in an even more basic form by the early Britons as an alternative to the circular hut. The advantage of this style was that it was easy to extend and, with a little thought and technology, to raise its height. The circular hut could not be extended either in length or height and so as a permanent building it had limited usage. It is true that many lasted well into the development period of the 'long-house', but eventually the box method of construction became the norm and the circular hut died out.

The Saxons were skilled shipbuilders and were well used to working with large timbers. They handled the axe and other woodworking tools with ease and their skill and technology soon had an effect on British carpentry, which underwent something of a revolution. The Saxons cut down massive trees in order to construct large buildings which more often than not took the form of impressive halls (see Fig 1).

At this time in Europe, man was building on a large scale and his buildings were constructed on a principle of measurement known as a 'bay'. The Saxon long-house would have been constructed in multiples of bays, and, in the same way that we may describe a house as having three, four or five bedrooms, the early timber-framed building could be described as having two, three or four bays. The bay divisions in a building can give a vital key to an overall understanding of the plan and construction of that building. We still use the term 'bay' today and it is a common term in the structural engineer's office where the overall structural design of a steel or concrete building is concerned.

The mechanical principle of a bay is as a collection point for

9

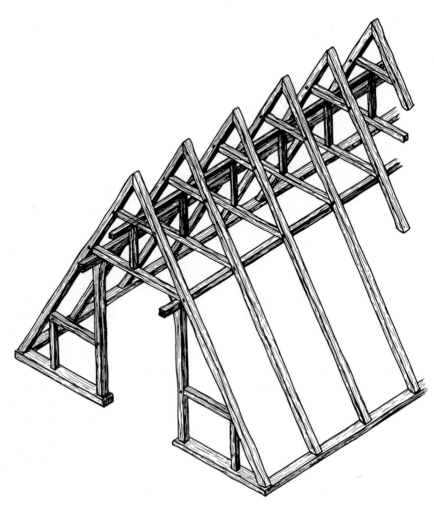

Fig 1 **Saxon hall.** The Saxons felled huge trees to provide hall buildings which were constructed along the lines of traditional ships. Saxon technology caused something of a revolution in British carpentry.

structural loadings which are transferred to the ground by means of posts and columns which make up the principal members of the building shell. It is important to remember that the bay division on a timber-framed building is also the point at which the front and rear walls are tied together. The method of tying the structure together may vary through types of frame construction, but provision of a tie-beam is a common basic principle, usually in a central position in the overall height of the building. The detailing of the tie-beam will vary with the style of frame, but generally three types of frame are common: the cruck, the post and truss, and the aisled. Originally, the plan of a house was simple: the bay represented a room, although it was common to have a two-bay room above two single-bay rooms at ground level. The effective length of a bay could also be reduced by the introduction of additional roof trusses which had the effect of shortening the structural bay.

The bay can vary in size from about 5ft (1.5m) – common in, say, a smoke bay – to about 20ft (6m) in a principal room. Most bays appear to be about 15ft (4.5m) in length, this being considered a sufficient space to house either a team of four oxen standing in two pairs or more commonly harnessed at the plough four abreast. The bay was a medieval unit of measurement and it has been suggested that the rod, which is about 5½yd (5m), is a derivation of the early medieval bay.

It has been mentioned that some bays might only be 5ft (1.5m) in length. Very short bays often house a smoke hood, smoke bay or, on occasion, a cross-passage. When the Saxons settled in Britain, they introduced a community philosophy to the native Britons. The Saxons had been used to the necessity of defence against marauding enemies and, as a result, had developed a strong community spirit and a sense of co-operation. They organised their farming on a joint basis and the philosophy over-spilled into their building. The principal tool of the Saxon carpenter was the axe and with it he cut huge areas of forest, concentrating on the largest trees with which to make the giant frames of his long-house. These buildings were designed to house not only the owner and his family, but also his animals and, if he were prosperous enough, his servants. Examples have been recorded around 70ft (21.3m) in length, although the normal length was likely to be about 40ft (12.2m).

The native Britons had been used to primitive dwellings, usually very temporary and crudely held together with lashing thongs at the ridges. By contrast the Saxons built on a massive scale. They cut and shaped their timbers, used elaborate joints to connect the timbers and had developed the method of pegging a joint to hold it fast once the connection had been made. The box frame had at last developed. The principal structural members of posts – tie-beams, wall plates and rafters – were jointed together into a box-like structure which, were it possible to lift, could have been picked up and turned upside-down or stood on its side. Oak was the timber predominantly used because of its weathering and strength characteristics. It was found to be a highly durable wood and demonstrates a remarkable resistance against the effects of dampness, insect and fungal attack. In short, it is immensely strong, does not rot easily or quickly and we now know that it has a remarkable resilience to fire: oak has a tendency to smoulder slowly and does not readily burst into flames. That is not, however, to say that many period timber-framed houses were not destroyed by fire. This surely must have been a great danger with open hearths, excessive draughts and thatched roofs.

As far as we can tell, the oak was not seasoned, mainly because the timbers used were so large that it was impractical. Immediately after felling, the timber was stood on end and did in fact season in situ in the building for which it was cut. It is difficult to be sure but it is believed that very few timbers stood for more than a few months, perhaps a year at the outside, before being used. The trees were cut with a large axe and split into baulks with an axe and iron wedges. An adze was used mainly to trim and square the wood for use on site. The length of timber used varied from area to area, and the size and quality of the trees available played an important part in the way in which the timber was worked. A usual length might be in the order of 10–20ft (3–6m), but in an important building lengths of 40–50ft (12.2–15.2m) were possible. Very long or over-large timbers were cut later by a substantial cross-cut saw with two handles, called a 'twart saw'. Timbers that needed to be cut along their length were cut with a pit saw operated by two men, one at ground level and one in the pit; the timber was laid over the pit and the men worked until it was eventually sawn in half.

The process of making a frame is in itself something for modern man to admire. Today we cut softwood trees with power saws and reduce the size of our cut timbers by means of electric or engine-driven circular or blade saws. Our technology provides for the treatment of timbers to be used in building by pressure injection or total immersion in preservative liquids, necessary because without such treatments the timber would rot. When freshly cut, the timber is wet and contains sap and other natural products which are unsuitable in the proposed use of the wood. It can take years for timber to dry naturally and season in this country, which is neither practical nor financially viable. For that reason we kiln-dry our wood and rapidly speed up the process which nature would have performed had the circumstances allowed.

The contemporary wall frame is constructed largely of softwood and connected with patent fixings. Other materials such as plywood, building paper, plasterboard and plastics are used in the overall construction, the frame of which is hidden under outer claddings and inner finishes. Outer claddings commonly include facing brickwork to give the general appearance of traditional brick construction.

The roof and wall frames of the period timber-framed house are an entirely different prospect. Oak trees were cut into suitable lengths for use as corner and principal posts, tie-beams and wall plates. The medieval carpenter cut joints into the wood and took considerable pride and care in doing so. He was a master of the joints: the mortice and tenon, the lap joint, the scarf joint in its different forms, the lapped-faced, halved, bridle, splayed and edge-halved scarf. He took a pride in cutting a complete joint and pegging it to perfection with tools that, by comparison to ours, were crude and unsophisticated.

WALL FRAMES

The typical medieval timber-framed house has walls with large open panels set between structural posts. When viewed in elevation, the principal horizontal timbers are as follows: at the base will be found the sill or sole plate, which may be of the continuous or interrupted type; at first-floor level is the bressummer, being the sill of the upper wall panel and spanning an opening to give support to the wall

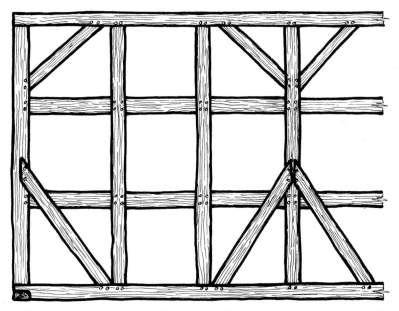

Fig 2 **Square panel and brace wall panel detail.** Braces between post and sill beam and post and wall plate. Square panels are of Western style.

13

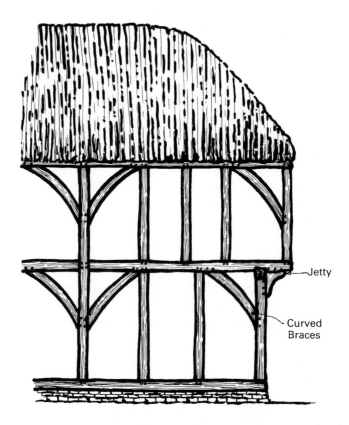

Fig 3 **Open wall panels with curved brace.** This example also is jettied at first-floor level. The braces are jointed from posts to mid rail and plates at roof level.

above; next is the wall plate upon which the roof structure sits, and may or may not be seen easily in elevation. The aforementioned timbers are usually braced with sharply elbowed or gently curved wall braces and these generally fall into two basic categories: the tension brace, which runs from the post down to the sill beam, and the arch brace, which runs from the post up to the wall plate (see Figs 2 and 3). Often other braces were added but mainly for decoration rather than structural stability. The arch brace is more common in the Midlands while the tension brace is more likely to be found in the South East, although there are rare instances where both can be seen on the same house. It is usual in a medieval building for walls to be framed in large open panels, often without intermediate studs or rails between the main structural posts, wall plates, bressummers and sole plates or sills. An important constructional detail in medieval house design is the brace. The arch brace rising from wall post to wall plate is the most common, but in parts of Kent it is usual for a window to be placed between two tension braces (that type being more common in Kent) and this is known locally as 'Kentish framing'.

Later, wall frames fell into three main categories: the Eastern, Western and Northern styles. The Eastern style (see Fig 4) comprised close studding set in tall and narrow panels, commonly seen in East Anglia. By the middle of the fifteenth century, this type of panel could be seen in better class buildings, usually in towns, all over the country. Later still, it became something of a status symbol because it displayed the free use of money in carpenters' time and the very expensive carpentry costs in oak.

The Western style (see Fig 2) displayed square panels and was used in poor quality buildings, internal partitions and other buildings such as barns and outbuildings. This style was quite common in the fifteenth century and can be seen in Surrey, Hampshire, Sussex and Berkshire.

The Northern, or decorated, style consists of square panels infilled with herring-bone, fleur-de-lis and star patterns. Also in the North

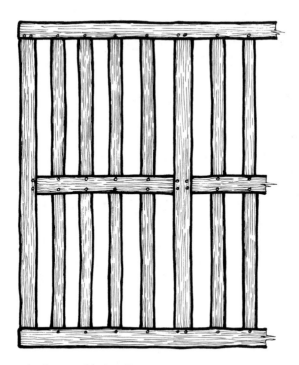

Fig 4 **Eastern style close studded wall panel.** Typical vertical panel design. Bracing was often curved between sill and post. A middle rail was commonly provided.

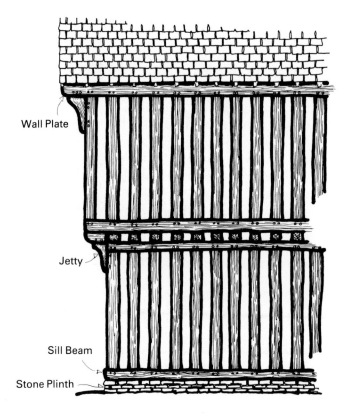

Wall Plate

Jetty

Sill Beam

Stone Plinth

Fig 5 Close studded wall panels shown here with a first-floor jetty. Note the jetty and stone plinth below the lower plate or sill beam.

it was common for vertical studs to rise from a sill, framed between the main structural posts, rather than from the sole plate (see Fig 6).

The Eastern and Western framing styles spread throughout the country but the Northern style tended to be very localised. For example, the square panel of the Western style undoubtedly originated around Gloucestershire in the fifteenth century, but examples can be seen over most of the country. The East Anglian close studding appears to have been the predominant style in that area for some two hundred years, but eventually its cost deterred further use and the style was lost.

When a wall panel was close studded, it was common for the studs to be at full storey height. The studs were jointed into the oak sole plates at ground level and into the bressummer and wall plates at upper levels. It was common for the studs to be placed at centres little

16

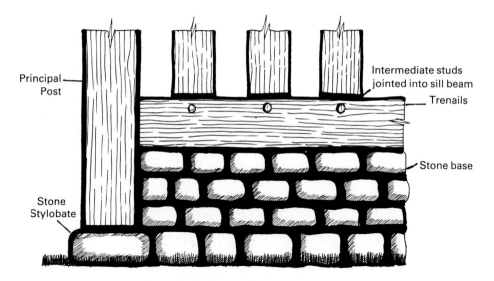

Labels in figure:
Principal Post
Intermediate studs jointed into sill beam
Trenails
Stone base
Stone Stylobate

Fig 6 **Northern style tenoned or interrupted sill beams.** This construction is common in northern areas. The corner posts bear directly onto stone stylobates and sills are tenoned into the sides of the principal posts.

more than the width of the stud, but after the sixteenth century, when timber became scarce and labour expensive, the spacing was increased. Buildings in the eastern counties, however, were designed in such a way that roof loadings were taken up by the external timber-framed side walls rather than the more normal transverse structural frames. It was mentioned earlier that buildings were sub-divided into bays. It can be added that in later times, bays were taxable. The eastern counties' building did not have the conventional bay, although the roof trusses did consist of slightly heavier timbers than in other parts of the building. The vertical studs were very often braced with tension-braces halved over the inside face of the inter-vening studs and hidden externally with plaster facings. The braces were usually cut from smaller timbers than the studs, although later it became common to use tension-braces of the same size as the studs, the two being firmly jointed together. In the eastern counties the principal truss and side purlin method of construction was not intro-duced until after about 1600.

In the western counties the post and truss is more common. The main posts are jointed at the base into the sole plate or sill beam and at the top into the wall plate. The principal posts are tied together across the building by means of main tie-beams; these also effectively stop the roof truss from spreading. Roof loadings were distributed

17

Plate 1 **A joint between sill beam and vertical post.** This joint is beginning to decay and lose structural strength.

via the purlins and wall plates to the principal posts and thus the ground. Longitudinal stability was given to the posts by means of arch bracings which commonly ran between the posts and the wall plate. In this way the wall panels remain non-structural as such and could therefore be constructed in lighter material. As in the eastern counties, it is possible to see close studding in the Westcountry but the western buildings often have an uninterrupted rail at first-floor level. A common detail in the East is storey-height vertical studding without a rail. It was mentioned earlier that the Northern style is commonly decorated with herring-bone, fleur-de-lis and star patterns. These were also employed in the sixteenth century when panels were enlarged to accommodate diagonal strutting as decoration. As time went on, and especially in the early part of the seventeenth century, panels became smaller and somewhat more regular in shape. The Northern style is essentially of the post and truss design, but the principal posts more commonly bear on stone stylobates than sole plates as do buildings in the West of England.

18

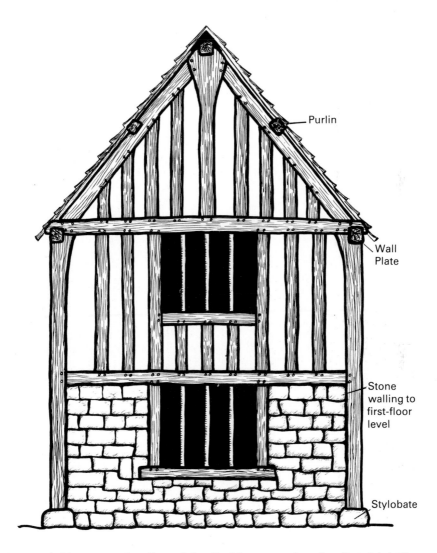

Purlin

Wall Plate

Stone walling to first-floor level

Stylobate

Fig 7 **Yorkshire truss and wall panel detail with stonework to first-floor level.** The principal post bears onto a stone stylobate. A first-floor rail is tenoned into the posts as shown in Fig 6.

The art of timber framing in the North can be referred to as the third school of English carpentry. It would seem that northern medieval carpenters looked at building styles in the East and the Westcountry and then took into account their own terrain and available materials. The resulting style has much in common with others but is always different and individual in some significant way. For instance, the post and truss frame of the West is jointed into the

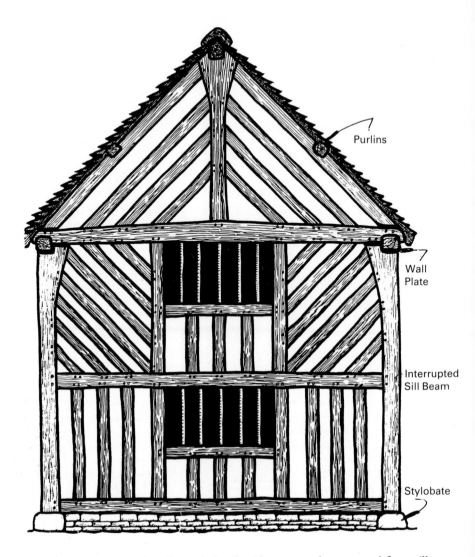

Purlins

Wall
Plate

Interrupted
Sill Beam

Stylobate

Fig 8 **Yorkshire truss and wall panel detail with stonework to ground-floor sill beam only.** Note the stylobates and interrupted sill beam at ground level. Typical of this area.

sill beam and receives loadings from the roof. The northern post and truss frame picks up roof loadings and transfers them via the principal posts to stone stylobates. The principal posts, however, still have sill beams, but in contrast to the western frame the sills are tenoned into the sides of the principal posts and are thus termed 'interrupted sills' (see Figs 6, 8 and 9).

Generally, the walls are framed with closely spaced studs often set

20

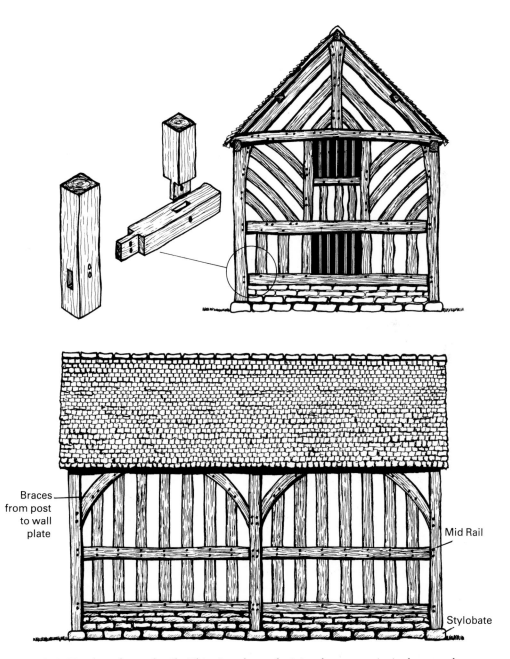

Fig 9 **Northern frame details.** This view shows the joints between principal post and sill beam and vertical stud with sill beam. This joinery is typical of the Northern School. See Fig 10 for enlarged view of mortice-and-tenon joint used here.

Braces
from post
to wall
plate

Mid Rail

Stylobate

out in two rows of unequal height, the bottom row frequently being the shorter in length. The studs are jointed into a rail, which spans the main posts, and curved arch-wind braces are tenon jointed into the posts and the wall plates in the top panels. Because of its availability, stone is widely used in the North, often as a facing to an earlier timber-framed building (see Fig 7).

Most people, if asked to describe a period timber-framed house, would say that it had black oak framing and white walls. They would probably suggest a thatched roof to complete the picture of the ideal country retreat. Very often the period timber-framed house is genuinely black and white, but this is usually as a result of someone's efforts with a tin of paint or stain. Before the nineteenth century, timber-framed houses were rarely painted black and the old oak was allowed, in fact, to weather naturally to that lovely silver-grey colour which is so attractive. It is possible that an early owner intent on painting his oak frame might have painted it ochre or earth red rather than black and that the panels were more likely to be of a light ochre in colour as a result of the impure limewash treatment known to have been given. In order to protect the building from penetrating dampness, the medieval owner would probably have coated the entire wall structure with limewash, including the frame, and this would have meant totally white or, rather, off-white buildings without any difference in colour in the frame.

WALL-FRAME JOINTS

The medieval carpenter prior to 1600 seldom adopted any other detail to hold a joint other than an oak peg or pin called a trenail. Because of the sheer strength needed in these apparently insignificant pieces of wood, they were always cut from the very heart of oak although, as has been already explained, the wood was unlikely to have been seasoned. It was possible to use iron nails and clamps, but these were generally far too costly for use in domestic building, and because the oak was unseasoned and so highly acidic, the chemical reaction of tannic acid on the metal would certainly have destroyed the strength of the fitting. The modern process of galvanising was unknown, but wrought metal was sometimes tinned as a protection against rust. It is highly likely that any clamp in a period timber-framed house, no matter how old-looking, is of comparatively recent date and has been installed to give added strength to the original heart-of-oak peg which may have failed as a result of differential

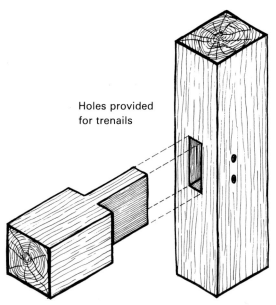

Holes provided
for trenails

Fig 10 **Unrefined mortice-and-tenon detail.** This joint is commonly used in the connection of a horizontal rail or sill to a vertical post.

settlement or extreme shrinkage. The heart-of-oak peg had an immense strength, and the medieval carpenter was able to utilise this strength in all his wall-panel and roof-truss joints. The medieval carpenter developed to an extremely high degree the art of making joints for all purposes, and all period timber-framed houses contain joints which are still sound even after several hundreds of years. There is little doubt that by the middle of the thirteenth century the medieval carpenter had a full range of joints at his disposal. Radio-carbon analysis has shown this to be the case. We know that the full range of mortice-and-tenon joints were used at this time as were lap-dovetail and scarf joints (see Figs 10–19).

The bridle scarf joint was commonly in use to join two sections of a wall plate, while the edge-halved and face-halved scarf joints may have been used in this context or to joint together bressummer or sill beams. The principle of the scarf joint is to join together two beams placed in line to form a continuous structural member. The scarf joint usually occurs near or adjacent to a principal post, and the position of the joint is often a key to the bay construction of the building. The lap-dovetail joint was very important in early medieval timber-framed building and is found in only a limited number of positions. This detail, which can be found in houses dating from the

23

thirteenth to the nineteenth centuries, is the main method of connection between the principal posts, the wall plate and the principal roof truss. The mortice-and-tenon joint is used extensively in wall-frame construction and occurs at the sill beam where the posts are tenoned to the sill, at the mid-rail joint with the posts, and the connections of post-with-brace and brace-with-plate. Even collars and tie-beams are connected with the mortice-and-tenon joint, always with pegs cut from heart of oak.

An understanding of joints in the period timber-framed house is an important criterion in dating. In describing the main joint details, it should be pointed out that because of regional differences it is only possible to show more common joint details, although the ones illustrated and described are those most likely to be encountered.

Lap joint The ordinary lap joint was an important part of early medieval construction when few other joints were used. In very early construction the mortice and tenon was not used and elements such

Plate 2 **A scarf repair to a collar purlin.** A carefully restored collar purlin using matching wood and a typical scarf joint.

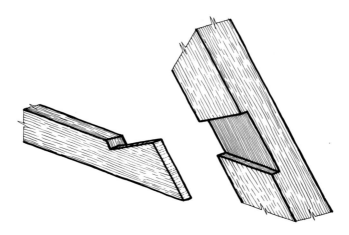

Fig 11 **Lap joint.** The lap joint is relatively rarely used in timber-framed buildings. Although significant in early medieval structures or later buildings they are mainly found as joints between collars and rafters and in cruck-frame construction.

as the medieval scissor brace were inserted after the main structural frame had been assembled. In this detail the mortice and tenon was impossible as it could only be used as a joint during, for instance, the assembly of the frame in the example given. The lap joint quite simply consisted of two pieces of timber from which about half the depth had been cut from each in a mirror fashion. To assemble the joint, the two pieces of timber were simply pressed together and pegged (see Fig 11).

Scarf joint This is an important group of joints when it is necessary to date a building since there are several varieties of scarf joint and they differ quite considerably over the centuries. The earliest is generally believed to be the splayed scarf which was common in the thirteenth and fourteenth centuries. The edge-halved scarf is generally believed to be the next main development, and this was a common detail from the fifteenth until the seventeenth centuries. The face-halved scarf joint was the next development, being common in buildings of post seventeenth-century date (see Plates 1 and 2).

Splayed scarf This joint is used where two ends of timber need to be connected. An example of such a situation could be a sill, bressummer or wall plate. One piece of timber is cut into a stepped pattern with the vertical faces of the step inclined into the timber

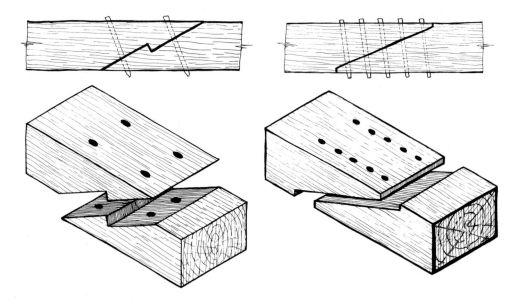

Fig 12 **Through-splayed and table scarf.** This joint is used to connect two pieces of timber end to end.

Fig 13 **Stop-splayed scarf with square under squinted abutments.** Yet another variation of the scarf, this was used to connect two timbers end to end. Note the number of fixing pegs.

rather like garden steps. The opposite piece is cut with the vertical faces inclined to notch into the first piece when the two timbers are laid one upon the other. The effect of the jointed timbers can be clearly seen in Figs 12, 13.

Edge-halved scarf The principle of this joint was similar to that of the lap joint. The edge-halved scarf would again be used to join two pieces of timber end to end, and perhaps the more common situation for this joint was in the wall plate. As mentioned, the joint was usually made near a main post or truss and its situation can often give an idea of the exact method by which the frame was constructed. The two ends of timber are cut into a halving and a male and female joint formed. The male joint is usually the top timber and is cut at the very end of the wood. The female joint is usually on the bottom timber and is set back from the end where it will correspond with the male when the joint is set. Exactly the same detail occurs with the bottom timber, but in mirror image so that each timber has both male and female members. Oak pegs are then inserted through the top and side of the joint (see Figs 14, 15).

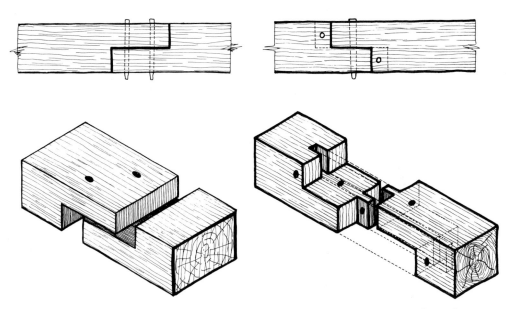

Fig 14 **Edge-halved scarf type 1.** This joint was used to join two sections of a wall plate or to join together bressummer or sill beams.

Fig 15 **Edge-halved scarf type 2.** The edge-halved scarf is used to join two pieces of timber end to end. A common situation for the joint is in wall plate construction. Common from the fifteenth century until the seventeenth century.

Face-halved scarf (also known as lipped face-halved scarf). In this joint the cuts are made on the vertical face rather than on the horizontal face as in the edge-halved scarf. The ends are each cut to form a tongue and a socket, the tongue at the end of the joint and the socket set back. The cuttings are in mirror image so that each timber inserts its tongue into the socket of the other. The joint is pegged through the socket, the tongue end usually in the centre halving for extra strength (see Fig 16).

Bridle scarf The two variations of bridle scarf are less common. In both types two ends of timber are cut, one into a socket and the other a tongue, and the tongue has a halving cut into it to allow it to fit into the socket in the other timber. In type A the tongue is cut with a splayed end; in type B it is cut with a square end. In both the usual detail is for the tongue and socket to be pegged twice for strength (see Fig 17).

Mortice-and-tenon joint This joint is the basis for all period timber-framing in this country. The joint is used in the connections of main

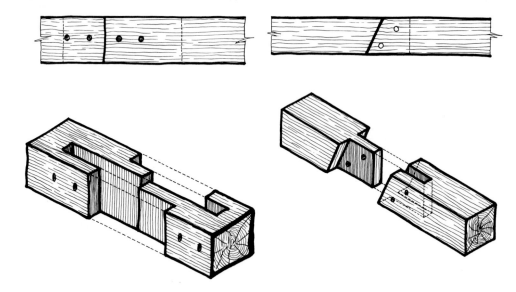

Fig 16 **Face-halved scarf joint.** Cuts are made on the vertical face rather than the horizontal. Each timber is cut in mirror image of the other and both halves are pegged together. This joint is often found in a wall plate connection.

Fig 17 **Bridle scarf.** This is a less common joint used to connect two ends of a wall plate. Scarf joints often appear near a vertical post and from their position a pattern of erection can sometimes be worked out. This joint was commonly used to join two sections of a wall plate.

posts to sills, bressummers to main posts, tie-beams to main posts and wind braces of both types to posts, wall plates and bressummers. The joint is cut either squarely across the timber, as in a connection between a bressummer and a post, or on an angle, as in the connection between a brace and a post or wall plate. When a connection is made between a vertical and horizontal member, the joint may be cut in an unrefined manner, being a simple tongue and slot pegged at the joint. As an alternative, the post being the slotted member may have a ledge or bracket provided at the base of the slot upon which the horizontal member may rest when the tongue is inserted into the slot. Again, the joint is pegged, often with two pegs. A further alternative is for the post to be cut into a ledge at the base of the slot, the slot cut on a splay in order that the tongued member may rest when the joint is connected. The entire joint is pegged with two pegs for strength (see Figs 18–22).

Tie-beam lap-dovetail joint One of the most important joints in the timber-framed house is the tie-beam lap-dovetail joint. This complex

28

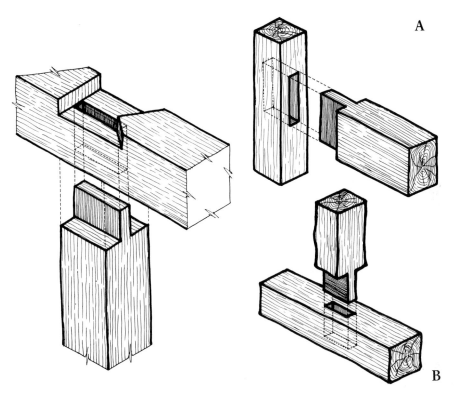

A

B

Fig 18 (above left) **Unrefined tenon detail.** This example connects a vertical post to a wall plate.

Fig 19 (above right) **Mortice-and-tenon joints. A) Post and beam connection. B) Post and sill beam connection.** This joint is the basis of all timber framing in this country. It is used in the connection of main posts to sills and bressummers to main posts.

Fig 20 (below left) **Mortice and tenon with shoulder.** The post is cut to form a ledge or shoulder upon which the end of the rail rests for extra support.

Fig 21 (below right) **Mortice and tenon with bracket.** The post is shaped to form a bracket upon which the rail end rests.

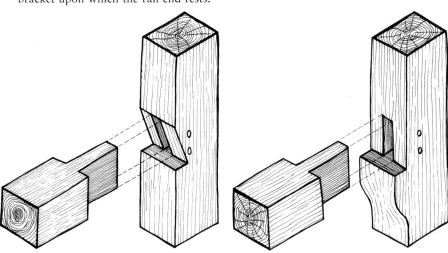

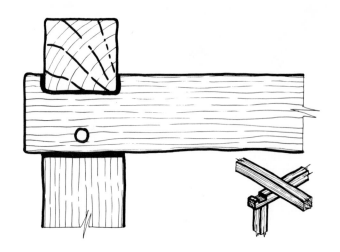

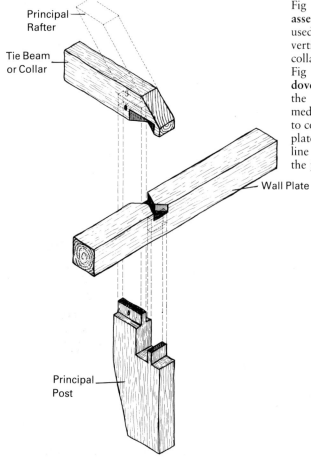

Principal Rafter

Tie Beam or Collar

Wall Plate

Principal Post

Fig 22 (above) **Reversed assembly joint.** A simple joint used at the connection of vertical post, wall plate and collar.

Fig 23 (left) **Tie-beam lap-dovetail joint.** This is one of the most important joints in medieval carpentry and is used to connect the main posts, wall plate and tie-beam. The broken line shows correct assembly of the joint.

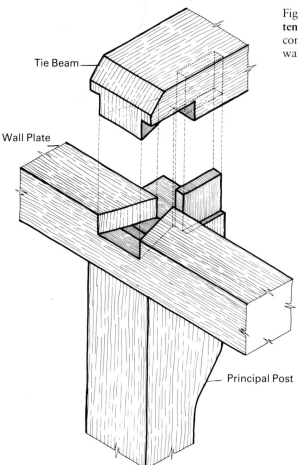

Tie Beam

Wall Plate

Principal Post

Fig 24 **Teazle tenon or jowl tenon.** This joint is used at the connection with principal post, wall plate and tie-beam.

example of medieval carpentry is used to connect the main posts, wall plate and tie-beam. An essential element in British carpentry traditions, this joint is a beautiful detail and its success long-lived. It appears in thirteenth-century buildings and was common in the nineteenth century. Because of the function of the joint it will not be seen in cruck buildings, but this type of structure will be dealt with later (see Fig 23).

The principle of the joint is as a vital connection between the main frame posts, the essential tie-beam, which is designed to stop the roof from spreading the walls, and the wall plate upon which the roof loadings are taken. For this reason the joint must be immensely strong, the whole joint being pegged after assembly. The common construction is as follows: the tie-beam is connected to the wall plate

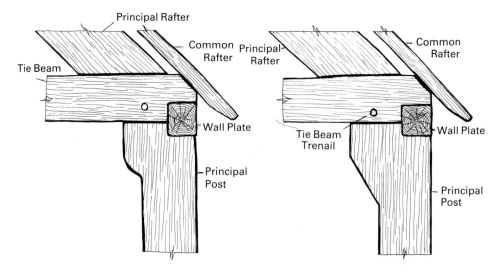

Fig 25 (above left) **Round jowl.** The jowl is an excess of timber formed at the top of a main post to give extra rigidity to the member. The early jowl is usually plain but during the sixteenth and seventeenth centuries it became an item for decoration. It died out during the eighteenth century.

Fig 26 (above right) **Splayed jowl.**

Fig 27 (below left) **Flared jowl.**

Fig 28 (below right) **Tapered jowl with rounded return edge.**

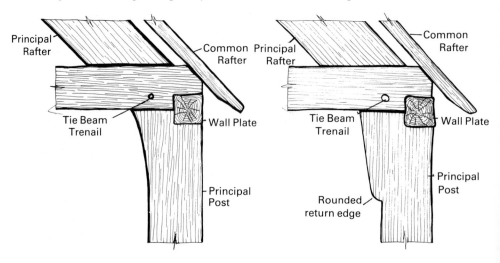

by a lap dovetail, although on some buildings this can be replaced by a bare-faced dovetail or one with a shoulder on one side only. The strains on this connection are enormous and often the joints open up as a result. To counteract this defect, the shoulder of the joint was sometimes housed as described under mortice-and-tenon joints (see

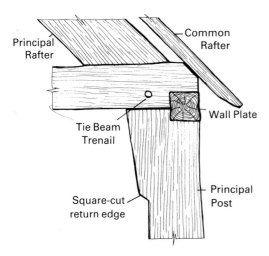

Principal Rafter

Common Rafter

Tie Beam Trenail

Wall Plate

Square-cut return edge

Principal Post

Fig 29 **Tapered jowl with square cut returned edge.**

p. 27). To facilitate a satisfactory job, the medieval carpenter often used an excess of timber to gain extra rigidity in the joint. This means that the main post was thickened out at the top into a member called a 'jowl' of which there were several types over the centuries (see Figs 24–9).

Jowls Flared, splayed and round jowls are common while tapered jowls are perhaps less so, but all served to give extra strength to the tie-beam lap-dovetail joint. The jowl was an intrinsic part of the lap-dovetail joint but was a highly visible part of the principal wall post and, as one might expect, received special treatment over the years. It is generally accepted that the jowl was common in the thirteenth century when its structural importance was respected, although expense was spared regarding decoration. The early jowl is usually a plain, totally functional member with extreme structural values. During the sixteenth and seventeenth centuries, it became fashionable to decorate important timbers and accordingly the jowl became the subject of ornamentation. Unfortunately, more time and money were spent on ornamentation and the jowl's structural capability declined until it died out altogether in the eighteenth century.

THE JETTY

A majority of buildings in towns and cities were timber framed up until the seventeenth century. The Great Fire of London in 1666 destroyed thousands of timber-framed houses, and the advent of

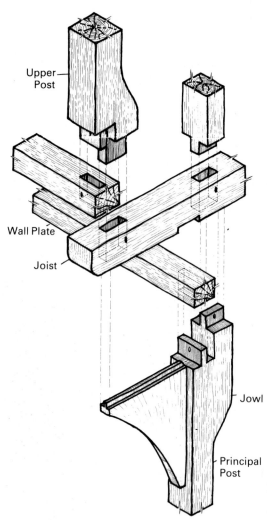

Upper Post

Wall Plate

Joist

Jowl

Principal Post

Fig 30 **Jetty, mainpost connection.** An elaborate system of joints used to provide a jetty overhang. As an indication of wealth, posts and beams were often elaborately decorated. The broken line shows correct assembly of the joint.

brick as a fashionable building material also helped to change ideas on construction methods. The carpentry details of urban timber-framed houses developed in much the same way as those in the country, but there were important constructional differences, especially in superior quality town buildings. It was more important to display affluence in the towns and, as a result, buildings tended to be decorated with elaborate framing and ornate panels. During the fifteenth and sixteenth centuries it was popular and indeed desirable for the upper storey of a building to project beyond the ground floor in a cantilever fashion. This method of construction was called jetty construction and became so popular that it was adopted in rural

Plate 3 (above left) **Continuous jetty.** This example is in Hampshire and has been carefully restored.
Plate 4 (above right) **Jetty details.** Part of a jetty showing the method of construction.
Plate 5 (right) **Jetty details.** See Plate 4.

areas on buildings of importance. As land prices rose, houses with more than two storeys were built to increase floor space. The function of the jetty was to create extra space at upper levels. Ground-floor sills or sole plates were laid and principal posts, studs and braces were morticed into each other to form a single-storey frame. The carpentry commonly adopted at the point of jettying is shown in Fig 30 and Plate 3.

As illustrated, the wall plate covering the front, or wall to be jettied, is morticed on to the principal posts and the first-floor joists are laid across the plate and morticed into the top of the principal post to lock the wall plate into position (see Fig 30). The amount by which the joists overhang will vary regionally and upon the style of the carpenter. The overhang may vary from 1ft to 2ft (30 to 60cm), but is most commonly 18in (46cm). As an indication of wealth it was common for the posts and beams to be elaborately decorated and often deep carvings appear on more important buildings. The upper cantilevered wall frame and panel was formed with a separate frame laid upon the lower. The principal posts were connected to the projecting floor joists by means of mortice-and-tenon joints inset to allow for the clasping of the sill from which the second-floor studs extend (see Plate 5). In order to strengthen the vertical posts, the splayed jowl was adopted more commonly. In the simpler jetties the end of the floor joists are exposed to view between the storeys, the upper-floor sill resting on the joists as described. In more elaborate buildings, the upper-floor sill is morticed on to the front edge of the

Plate 6 **Jetty bracket details.** This example is at the Weald and Downland Open Air Museum at Singleton, Sussex. It is particularly well restored and presented in the original form.
Plate 7 **Corner jetty detail.** From the same building; note the restored newer timber and the perfection of match achieved.

Plate 8 **Continuous jetty.** An example from Hampshire particularly well restored earlier this century.

joists, thus concealing them from view. In this detail the sill beam is often decorated as an indication of wealth and affluence. In all cases the principal posts are morticed to the upper sills as described.

It was common in more important buildings for the window mullions of lower-floor projecting windows to be tenoned into the underside or soffit of the jetty sill beam above. There are now unfortunately very few buildings in existence where this detail can be seen, but evidence of it exists in the old mortice slots and peg-holes in a number of buildings still standing (see Plate 6). Dependent upon the wealth of the owner, a building might have two or even three jetties and extend to perhaps four floors, although there are relatively few such buildings standing. A very important building might have a jetty on all four main elevations while another of less importance on only two or three elevations (see Plate 7). Generally, this was regarded as

Plate 8a (above left) **Bracing at first-floor level.** A well restored example of framing on the Hampshire–Surrey border.

Plate 8b (above right) **Jetty detail on a Wealden house.** Note the scantling of timber used on this example from Sussex.

Plate 8c (left) **Jetty details.** A part tile-hung frame at the Weald and Downland Museum at Singleton, Sussex.

an indication of status and was thus designed to be seen by the general public. They in turn received some benefit because a measure of protection was offered from the elements in towns and cities. It gave extra space to the upper floors of a building and this became very appreciable when the building was of more than two levels. A later post-medieval development of the jetty was the jetty house which became common in the sixteenth and seventeenth centuries. In this construction, detailing was similar to that of the older single-jetty building but it extended for the entire length of the building which might have public usage. Very often the local market hall or guildhall was constructed in this way (see Plate 8).

OUTSHUTS

An outshut or outshot is an extension to a building under a lean-to or cat-slide roof. The writer's own fifteenth-century house had an outshut built on to the original rear-wall frame. The front and gable ends of the building were faced in brickwork and there is strong evidence in the first-floor joists that in its original form the first floor was jettied on the front elevation. The village in which the house stands was very important in the medieval period and the exact positioning of the house in the village was a key factor in its design

Fig 31 **Outshut (outshot) detail.** This later outshut to a timber-framed house is walled with 225mm (9in) brickwork. Note the 'cat-slide' roof over the added-on portion.

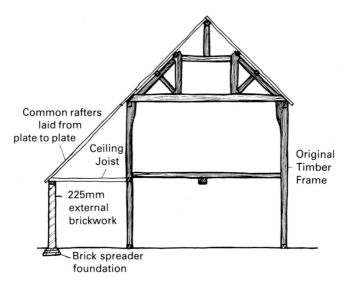

39

and construction. It is clear from an examination of the house that its size was increased during the late fifteenth and early sixteenth centuries. The wall-frame details differ slightly at one end and the roof construction changes from high quality to a lesser standard. The need for increased internal space was partially satisfied by the removal of the old ground-floor front wall and jetty which, from the clear markings on the massive oak floor joists, overhung by about 1ft 10in (55cm). Extra space was gained at the rear of the house by construction of an outshut.

Most timber-framed houses were laid out on a simple rectangular plan. A typical house was divided into bays, but this basic shape was somewhat restrictive in the event of an extension since it might not be possible simply to add another bay and effectively increase the length of the building by a further 15ft (4.5m) or so. The alternative was to build at the rear of the house on the ground floor only and to continue the existing roof coverings over the new extension. This meant that when viewed in profile, the roof, which is at normal height in the front at eaves' level, changes at the rear extending to below ground-floor ceiling height. In the writer's house, the outshut used to be a dairy in the original bay sector and the later second bay sector became an inner hall with an oak staircase and a dining-hall. From anywhere in the outshut the entire original oak rear-wall framing was visible and made a wonderful feature. In the dining-hall we removed a substantial amount of very poor quality softwood framing which held up a defective lath and plaster ceiling. This ceiling had a height of about 6ft 6in (2m) and appeared to encase some more substantial timber. It is easy to remember the excitement felt one cold Saturday afternoon when we plucked up enough courage to demolish the ceiling and, when the dust had settled, saw for the first time the beautiful original lath and plaster wall panels extending up to the old wall-plate level. The quality of the joinery was superb and the installation of the Victorian ceiling had in effect shut the entire construction away in a dark but well-ventilated cupboard.

Not only did we have original wattle-and-daub panelling but also an early window neatly boxed in for some reason that cannot be explained. We later found another window in the rear wall of the main bedroom which was in the older part of the house, and this effectively overlooked the later dairy which we made into a farm-house kitchen. The more substantial timber apparently covered by the Victorian ceiling in the dining-hall turned out to be a massive bressummer which bore into the original corner post with a huge mortice-and-tenon joint. Suffice it to say that all the timbers in this area were exposed and created a feature of which we were justly more than proud.

The roof was in a cat-slide style, being simply an extension of the original structure, which was a common feature on houses of this basic construction. It is often difficult to tell whether an outshut is an original part of the structure or whether, as in our case, it has been added on at a later date. One reasonably certain way of telling is the purpose for which the outshut has been used. It is true that over the years the use may have changed, but generally the presence of a main staircase in the outshut indicates that it has been built on at a later date. It is, however, also common for the outshut to have been added to, or even demolished and rebuilt in a larger form, and under these circumstances dating can be difficult. Evidence to suggest that this has happened may be found in the principal posts where mortices might be discovered, indicating the connecting points with old tie-beams (see Fig 31).

PRE-FABRICATION AND ASSEMBLY OF THE TIMBER FRAME

We have discussed the various types of joint commonly used to make connections essential in the structural stability of the period timber-framed house. The work was carried out by highly skilled carpenters using comparatively simple tools but in a most effective way. Trees were initially felled with a narrow axe, although an extra large tree might necessitate use of the broad axe to cut a slot around the tree so that the narrow axe could be used to finish the job and cut the solid heartwood. Larger trees were split into baulks with hammers, wedges and axes and the baulks were trimmed with the medieval adze. The timber was cut with a two-handled cross-cut saw called a 'twart saw' or with a pit saw operated by two men, one standing at ground level and the other standing in a deep pit, each holding an end of the saw with the beam spanning the pit.

This must have been incredibly hard work and most of it was done in the carpenters' or framing yard, 'framynplace' as it was called (see Plates 9, 10, 11). Very often the framynplace was some distance from the site where the house was to be built. The medieval carpenter did not usually work the timber on site, although this is a popular mis-conception today. Another frequent misconception is the ships' timbers fallacy. Many people are convinced that their houses are con-

Plates 9-11 **The modern framing yard.** Views at a framing yard in Sussex. The contemporary equivalent of the medieval carpenters' yard.

structed of ships' timbers. This fallacy appears to have grown out of the belief that tie-beams, often very large in section and cambered, are reused deck bulkhead timbers. One client was absolutely convinced that his house was built from ships' timbers; the house had two bays and the principal posts, rafters and tie-beams were very substantial and quite obviously reused timber. It was very difficult to convince him that the house, which he believed dated from the early sixteenth century, did, in fact, date from very much later and had been built from second-hand timber, probably from a larger but much older house. This explained the extra large sections of timbering, the inconsistency of carpenters' marks and the fact that just about every length of timber had apparently meaningless mortice slots indicating another usage.

Many early timber-framed houses were demolished and the materials reused in much the same way that we do today. My client, however, said that the Portsmouth naval shipyards were in relatively close proximity and that timber ships were scrapped there, the timbers salvaged and sold to builders for the purpose of constructing timber-framed houses. One cannot say that my client was wrong, but can say that the old meaning of 'ships' timbers' was probably an expression of the quality of the wood and not its exact usage. As a contemporary example, marine plywood is used to make hull skins in boatbuilding, but that does not mean that all marine plywood is gained from scrapped small boats. The material is produced for its strength and characteristics in boatbuilding, but can also be used happily in the construction of a house.

Returning to the framynplace, the freshly cut oak tree was usually not given a chance to season. Principal beams and posts were formed

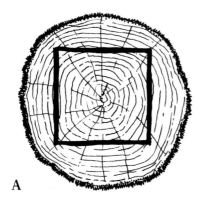

Fig 32 **Raw timber sections. Three ways of cutting a log to provide suitable timber.** A) Mainposts and beams. B) Structural studs, rails etc. C) Minor timbers, floor boards etc.

A

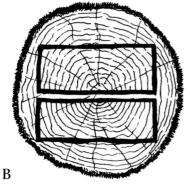

B

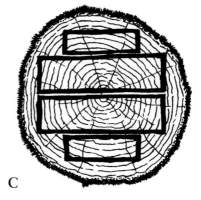

C

out of heartwood, the timber being squared off with the axe or adze (see Figs 32a–b). Smaller beams were cut from a log squared off with the adze and then sawn down the length with a pit saw. Studs and planks were formed out of a log cut several times from end to end, the rough edges being squared off with an adze (see Fig 32c). This exercise was called 'slabbing'. The timbers would vary in length according to the age of the tree and the use to which they were to be put. Principal beams were likely to be in the order of 15ft (4.6m) to 20ft (6m), although this could vary with circumstances. It is quite common to see larger beams and in the author's fifteenth-century house the main beautifully moulded and original trimmer achieved a length of over 40ft (12.2m). The writer recently inspected a barn which had a massive principal beam in excess of 50ft (15.2m) in length. Such a timber created headaches for the carpenter, not least because of its extreme weight and hardness. The writer has often wondered how such a timber was eased into position without the aid of a modern crane. Other smaller timbers such as poles, staves, laths and pegs were cleft and split, being an easier and quicker method than sawing. Timbers were worked with the axe, adze, planes, chisels, mallets, hammers and the breast auger.

Partly to economise on timber, a beam would be cut from the smallest possible log, and very often on lower specification houses the bark and softer sapwood was left exposed on the lower face and perhaps on the edge of the timber. Rafters were probably cut from smaller trees which had not necessarily grown straight. The method used was to cut the tree from end to end and thus form a pair of rafters. Floor joists were formed from larger trees in much the same way, the cleft face pointing upwards to give a relatively flat surface on which to lay the floorboards. In better quality houses the joists were likely to be sawn from larger trees, and in my own house the joists were chamfer moulded (see Figs 75, 76, 77, pages 155–6), 7 × 7in (17.5 × 17.5cm) at about 10in (25cm) centres. This meant that if another joist had been laid between, the ceiling would have been solid to a depth of 7in (17.5cm) plus the thickness of the floorboards. A more common joist size is 8 × 6in (20 × 15cm), although this does vary from area to area. When talking about cambered ships' timbers we referred to a client's belief that his tie-beam was a reused deck bulkhead; in fact, curved oak trees were especially selected to make tie-beams in exactly the same way as they were selected to make the curved blades of a cruck frame.

When constructing a timber suspended floor in a modern house, the carpenter lays 7 × 2in (17.5 × 5cm) or 8 × 2in (20 × 5cm) softwood floor joists in an upward position so that the vertical face is the larger dimension. The timber is obviously stronger laid this way rather than flat. The medieval carpenter, however, laid his more substantial oak joists with the larger dimension flat, or in other words turned through 90° from the modern method. The medieval timbers were stronger than they needed to be and did not deflect to any great extent, but the simple logic for this construction was that the top face of the joist may have been heartwood and therefore immensely strong. It was also likely to be a flat hewn face more convenient to fix upper floors to. The modern softwood joist might be cut from any section of a much weaker and inferior log (see Fig 32).

In the framynplace the prepared timbers were laid out and the joints cut accordingly. The entire wall panel was assembled on the ground and the joints eased or adjusted as necessary. Each component part was marked at this time so that when taken apart it could be easily identified. In this way every joint was purpose made, every mortice had a tenon tailor-made to fit it and every completed joint was ready drilled to take a prepared heart of oak peg for final on-site fixing. The component parts of the frame were lifted on to waggons and transported to the site of assembly. It is very likely that some timbers travelled considerable distances to the site and that river links were used to transport heavier timbers. For example, the great roof timbers of Westminster Hall were prefabricated at Farnham and transported by cart to London. On smaller frames, it may have been possible to fix certain elements of a frame together in the framynplace, to the extent of hammering home the oak locking pegs. It might have been possible, given enough pairs of willing hands, to erect a frame in one piece, but this would have caused considerable difficulty owing to the sheer weight of the structure (see Plates 12–17).

Most buildings of any reasonable size were erected in stages, with timbers placed in position one by one. The carpenter would have calculated the order in which timbers were erected, and this pattern was followed strictly. Failure to follow the order would have caused all sorts of problems with mortice-and-tenon joints not able to connect and rails and braces left out. The order of assembly can often be calculated today, and it was mentioned earlier that the scarf joint positions are a likely key to the order of construction. While many timbers could be carried by a small number of men, some form of rigging was necessary for heavier materials. We know that ropes and

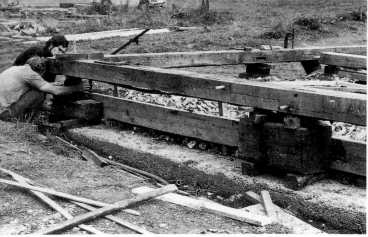

Plate 12 (above left) **Erection of the frame.** Underpinning the frame to get the sill beam level prior to wall frame erection.

Plate 13 (above centre) **Erection of the frame.** The wall frames are in the process of erection.

Plate 14 (above right) **Erection of the frame.** Windbraces and windows are fixed to one elevation before the next horizontal member is laid.

Plate 15 (below left) **Erection of the frame.** First-floor members are added to one wall and tie-beams jointed into place.

Plate 16 (below centre) **Erection of the frame.** A principal member is lifted into place by a modern crane.

Plate 17 (below right) **Erection of the frame.** The building is half complete. Note the use of the modern crane to lift heavy members.

pulleys were used and it is possible that shear-legs aided the lifting of extra heavy timbers.

CARPENTERS' MARKS

Large frames required a sophisticated identification system and this was achieved by the use of carpenters' marks. When in the framyn-place, the timbers going to form a structural frame were numbered to identify the members. The system most commonly adopted was based on Roman numerals, the marks being cut with a scribe or chisel to the upper face of the member. A tag was used to identify the frame. The system was based on combinations of I, V and X, though the V was sometimes inverted. When X and V were used together, or when two or more Xs were used together, it was common for one cross cut to serve them. The marks show the number of a member in

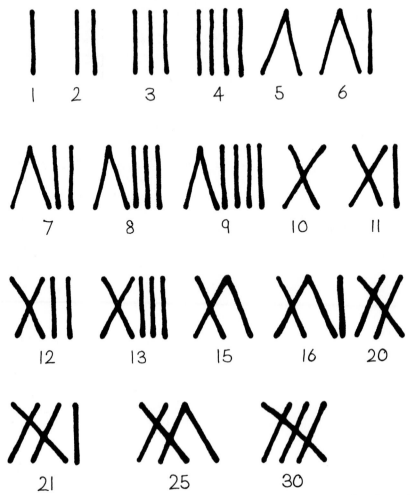

Fig 33 **Carpenters' marks.** Used to identify timber members at the time of construction.

the frame while the tag is to identify the frame to which the member belongs. There was also another system of numbering, although this was only used on cross-frames. Each frame was given a number which was marked on the main structural components: the principal posts, sills, bressummers and trusses. A tag was usually added to the mark to identify right from left and thus avoid confusion on site. The carpenters' marks on a period timber-framed house are a great source of interest to the building surveyor and layman alike who, if he is diligent enough, can work out the structure of the building and ascertain the extent of original work (see Fig 33).

48

The cruck is generally regarded as one of the earliest types of timber frame and it is a popular opinion that its use was limited to the poorer classes. We now know that this was not the case and that many early surviving crucks from the thirteenth and fourteenth centuries are of a superior construction, using superior timber to those more numerous of later date. It is possible that the cruck reached a peak of development in the Welsh Marches and the Midlands where it was used in the construction of medieval barns and halls. The cruck was not therefore solely for the upper classes, and many poorer quality structures using less substantial timbers must have disappeared over the years. The main principle of the cruck is rigidity and simplicity which, together with the use of oak and other hardwoods such as black poplar, created a practical, strong and most attractive structure. Most of the early surviving crucks are of a basecruck type in which the cruck frames rise from the ground and are truncated below the apex. The frames are joined together at the end of the truncation with a collar or tie-beam which traverses the building. Upon this is affixed the roof structure.

The cruck frames consist of two halves of a tree trunk, ideally curved. The whole length of the trunk is sawn in half and the two halves are laid against each other to form an arch. In the most primitive form, the frames were of lightweight section, and the lower end at ground level would have been charred to prevent the ingress of rising water in the wood grain, a cause of rot. A baulk of timber laid vertically in this way without some form of protection at lower level would rot very quickly, thus allowing the structure to fail. This must have happened in many cases before the early builders realised the fault and were able to promote a cure.

In the early frames the collar or tie-beam was probably lashed to the cruck frames in order to make a connection. The method of fixing probably varied, dependent upon the section of the crucks as some were gently curved, some were actually straight and others formed with an elbow. The principle of the cruck is similar to that of post-and-cruck construction in that the roof loadings are transferred to the ground by means of structural transverse frames. The overall concept is structurally sound and can be seen in portal frames formed of steel and concrete used today in industrial and agricultural buildings throughout the country.

In the smallest of buildings, two sets of crucks would be used, one at each end, to form two gable walls. Larger structures would simply add extra frames at bay centres. As described, a bay is approximately 16ft (4.9m) in length, although this dimension varies. At the very apex a lighter pole called the ridge piece would be used and at a lower point on either side of the roof planes parallel timbers called purlins would be placed. These effectively tied the cruck frames together. The purlins gave support to the outer roof coverings which were formed of heather, brush and straw thatch. The external walls were of a non-load-bearing type, all loadings being transferred to the end crucks for structural rigidity. The cruck timbers in a sawn state are commonly known as blades. The bottom ends of the earlier cruck blades were burned to protect them from the effects of dampness, but a later development was the provision of a stone base known as a stylobate upon which the base of a blade rested for protection (see Figs 38–40). An even later development was the provision of a stone plinth upon which a timber sill plate was laid. This ran for the perimeter of the building and was jointed at the corners. The bottom ends of the cruck blades were then cut and jointed into the sill plate.

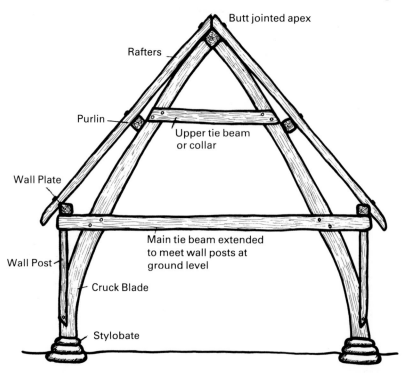

Fig 34 **Cruck with vertical wall studs jointed to cruck blades and butt jointed apex.** The main tie-beam is extended to carry the wall plate. Vertical wall studs are jointed with the underside of the tie-beam.

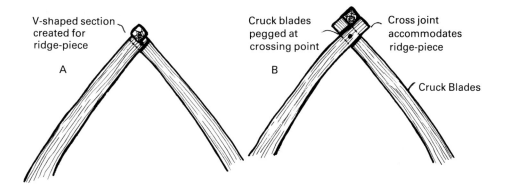

V-shaped section
created for
ridge-piece

A

Cruck blades
pegged at
crossing point

Cross joint
accommodates
ridge-piece

B

Cruck Blades

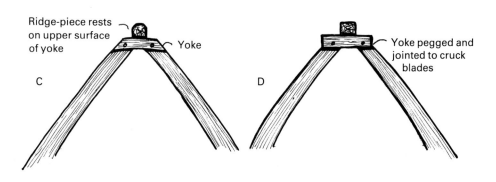

Ridge-piece rests
on upper surface
of yoke

Yoke

C

Yoke pegged and
jointed to cruck
blades

D

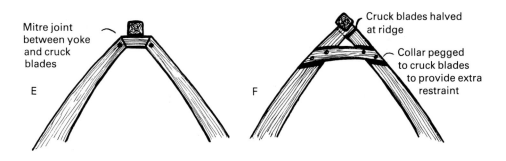

Mitre joint
between yoke
and cruck
blades

E

Cruck blades halved
at ridge

Collar pegged
to cruck blades
to provide extra
restraint

F

Fig 35 **Typical ridge joints in cruck construction.** Six variations of apex joint at the ridge where cruck blades connect.

This detail provided protection on two counts: first, the stone plinth acted as protection against rising dampness, effectively acting as a damp-proof course; secondly, the provision of horizontal timbers transmitted dampness away from the end grain of the vertical members and thus offered a very thorough second protection against rot.

There are several methods of connecting the upper ends of the cruck blades and these vary from building to building.

The butt detail In this method the blade ends were cut to a square section. The two lower edges were joined together in a butt fashion and the suitably shaped ridge piece was dropped into an L-shape formed by the squared-off ends of the blades (see Fig 34).

The housed detail In this method the ends of the cruck blades were cut off squarely in a similar fashion to the butt detail. In order to give additional contact with the blade ends, the lower corners were also cut with a splay so that a greater area of wood was connected. In a similar manner to the butt detail, the ridge piece was dropped into the top to complete the joint.

The halving detail This method adopted the principle of the halving joint. The blade ends were cut into a halving so that the removed end section of timber matched the end section of the ridge piece to be laid therein. Both blades were cut on the same edge so that when they were placed in the designed position they formed a mounting for the ridge piece (see Fig 35a).

Crossed detail In this method the blades were set so as to cross at the ridge in a manner resembling scissors. The crossing joint was pegged for rigidity. The ridge piece was then laid into the apex of the cross to complete the joint (see Fig 35b).

Yoke detail This cruck ridge detail was slightly more complicated. The blades were cut to a set length and shaped to the top face of a small collar called a yoke, which was affixed across the blades and thus pegged into position. The ridge piece simply sat or lay on the top face of the yoke collar, with all loadings taken by the joints; the cruck blades may have borne a small amount from the ridge piece resting directly on them (see Fig 36a).

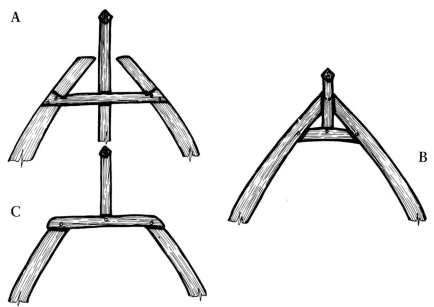

Fig 36 **Typical cruck ridge details.** A) Yoke and upstand. B) Yoke. C) Tenoned upstand.

Tenoned upstand detail In this detail the cruck blades were cut to a length by which they almost touched at the apex. A collar or yoke was tenoned between the blades almost at ridge level. A ridge upstand, a short vertical timber, was tenoned into the yoke at the centre and the blades were tenoned into the side at the upstand and pegged into place. The top edge of the upstand was cut into a bird's mouth, being a V-shaped cut, and the ridge piece laid into it to complete the joint (see Fig 36b).

Yoke and upstand detail This joint is a somewhat weaker variation of the tenon upstand in that the cruck blades are cut to the shape of the top edge of the yoke, which is tenoned and pegged as in the ordinary yoke type. The upstand is tenoned and pegged into the yoke in a central position, as in the tenoned upstand detail, but the upstand is not in any way given lateral support from the cruck blades. The ridge piece was cut to fit in the bird's mouth in the top face of the yoke upstand (see Fig 36c).

In all the connections discussed, the common factor is the ridge piece that runs from one cruck blade set to another. The length of the building would determine the number of blade sets provided. In a

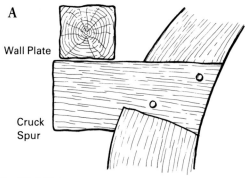

A

Wall Plate

Cruck
Spur

Fig 37 **Cruck spur details.**
A) Cruck spur supporting wall
plate. B) Cruck spur connected
to wall posts and rails.

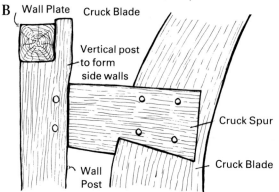

B Wall Plate   Cruck Blade

Vertical post
to form
side walls

Cruck Spur

Cruck Blade

Wall
Post

Fig 38 **Full(er) open cruck
truss also known as a raised
cruck.** Note the stone stylobate
base and curved tie-beam. The
ridge is of a plated yoke type.
See Fig 35 for enlarged view.

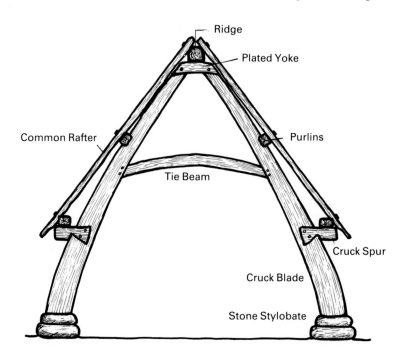

Ridge

Plated Yoke

Common Rafter

Purlins

Tie Beam

Cruck Spur

Cruck Blade

Stone Stylobate

similar manner to the ridge, wall plates and purlins also ran from blade set to blade set.

In some crucks the external walls were formed of timber; when this occurred the internal tie-beams were extended until the ends were directly above the feet of the cruck blade and the sill. In the full or open cruck, typical in the sixteenth and seventeenth centuries, side posts were mounted vertically from the sill up to a point just less than one-third of the overall height of the building (see Figs 37–8, 41). The posts were tied back to the cruck blade by means of a device known as a 'cruck spur'. This was typically a piece of timber, oak or other similar hardwood, to the shape of a tapered tenon, the widest edge being on the inside of the joint to avoid the possibility of the joint being pulled apart laterally. At the other end the cruck spur was cut to form a mortice-and-tenon joint with the vertical side post. When the joint was assembled, the spur rigidly held the side posts to the cruck blade and fixing pegs were inserted through the joints at both the blade and wall-post ends. At a central point, the vertical post would usually be divided by a horizontal bar which would aid support for the side-wall panels.

At the top of the vertical side posts, the wall plate was affixed, usually sitting in a cut-out socket provided for this purpose. Intermediate rafters would be placed at suitable centres between the cruck blades and these were supported on purlins which were normally cut into the cruck blades to form a small socket (see Figs 38, 40). At each joint, pegs were used to hold the structure firmly together.

The number of purlins used on either side of a roof plane varies from building to building. Usually, one purlin was placed near the centre or two spaced out at one-third and two-thirds intervals along the length of the span between the wall plate and the ridge (see Figs 40–1). In the full or open cruck it was common for only one collar or tie-beam to be provided, this being at a height of at least two-thirds the total height of the building. The collar was commonly tenoned into the inside edge of the cruck blade and may well have had additional braces to tie it back to a lower point in the cruck blades. From inside the effect would be most pleasing and the collar would appear to be part of an arched structure. The ridge varies from region to region and the blades may well have been yet again tied at the ridge by means of a further much smaller collar or tie. Usually this would also be tenoned into the inside edge of the cruck blades.

Dependent upon size and shape of the cruck blades, there is a variable detail concerning the purlins and blades. In some cases,

55

especially where two purlins have been used on either side of a roof plane, an additional timber may have been adopted to effectively flatten out the natural shape of the cruck blade. Normally, the base of the additional timber is tenoned into the top of the side wall posts immediately adjacent to the wall plate. The timber then rests on the cruck blade, although it is only a half or two-thirds the length of the span between the top of the wall plate and the ridge. At the point where it rests on the blade, it is pegged to the blade timber and the lower purlin is cut into a socket in the timber and pegged. The common rafters then bear on the lower purlin which is not directly connected to the cruck blade and to the upper purlin which is directly connected (see Fig 40). At the base of each set of blades and running the perimeter of the building is the sill plate, and in addition a ground plate runs across the building in line with the cruck blades to stop outward spread at the base of the frame.

Besides the open full cruck there is a variation in the closed full cruck where a further collar is added just below wall-plate level, spanning the building from one blade to the other (see Fig 39). In the North of England crucks are less developed than in other areas; the

Fig 39 **Yorkshire cruck frame.** The closed full cruck includes an additional tie-beam just below plate level.

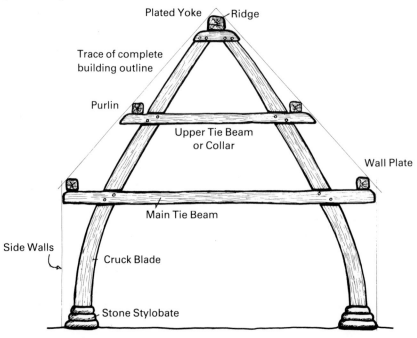

Plated Yoke — Ridge

Trace of complete building outline

Purlin

Upper Tie Beam or Collar

Wall Plate

Main Tie Beam

Side Walls

Cruck Blade

Stone Stylobate

blades are often roughly hewn and little attention paid to finer detailing. One possible reason for this is that the frames were often clad in stone, hiding the members from immediate view. In the Midlands, however, a cruck structure commonly had timber-framed walls and attention to finish is thus more notable. It is quite easy to see a direct line of development in northern crucks owing to the crudity of carpentry and joinery. In the northern cruck it is common for a roughly hewn frame to be set on stylobates and linked at the ridge in the yoke detail (see Fig 38).

Two collars are often affixed to the cruck blades by means of pegged halving joints. The collars or tie-beams would usually be affixed at about one-third and two-thirds intervals along the cruck blade. The collars are cut so that the bottom tie-beam end is approximately on line with the base of the cruck blade. The upper collar is cut with a projection which sets it on line with an imaginary edge developed between the ridge piece and the bottom tie-beam end. The wall plate is then affixed to the top face of the main collars as shown in Fig 39. The top collar acts as a structural base for the purlin which spans from this to the next cruck blade set.

The full cruck is often called a 'raised cruck' because the base of the blade is often contained within a wall and may be well above outside ground level. The base cruck rises from ground level and the blades are usually cut substantially below the ridge and tied together with a collar or tie-beam. This is the main means of support for the roof structure. Most surviving examples of the base cruck are fourteenth century in origin, while surviving raised crucks seem to be somewhat later (see Fig 38).

A number of surviving crucks can be found in cottages, houses and barns throughout the country. Those of fourteenth- and fifteenth-century origin are usually in houses or other buildings of high quality, and the timbers used are substantial in size and strength. Surviving examples of poor cruck construction date almost entirely from the sixteenth, seventeenth and eighteenth centuries; early crucks built to a poor standard and of inferior materials inevitably decayed long ago.

At the lowest level the poorer cruck was, according to contemporary documentation, 'a very common structure'. It is unlikely to have been built on a medieval hall plan, and the bays would have housed the owner, his family and animals under the meanest of conditions. In the South and the Midlands most crucks are of medieval origin. During the sixteenth century, cruck construction became less common and one possible reason for this was the need of heavy section curved oak timbers in the shipbuilding industry.

A further variation of the cruck is the raised base truncated type. The detail around the base is similar to that of the ordinary raised base cruck. The main difference between the two is that the blades of the truncated type are cut at a point level with the upper collar or tie-beam. Where the cruck was of an open type, there was no provision for a lower collar and the purlins were simply trenched or let into the outside edge of the cruck blade. Alternatively, in some cases purlins may rest on top of the truncated blade where it has been tenoned into the top collar.

Where the cruck is of a closed type, the lower purlins and plates may rest on the extended lower collar or tie-beam. At the apex the roof planes are continued to ridge level but the curved part of the cruck is not extended; this terminates at upper collar level. A further small collar after the yoke may be adopted at the ridge point (see Fig 39).

A further variation of the cruck frame is the upper cruck. In this construction with side walls, a substantial lower collar or tie-beam is used to prevent roof spread and lateral movement in the wall panels. Wall plates are connected to the upper edge of the wall posts and the end of the main collar. A cruck frame is then formed with the lower blade ends morticed into the top end of the collar at a point inside the external wall posts. The cruck blades are developed up to ridge height and are commonly given a cross-ridge detail as previously described (see Fig 35b).

An upper collar of a smaller section is usually provided to form an A-frame structure in the cruck blades and thus prevent lateral movement at this level. The central purlins are not normally trenched into the outside edge of the cruck blade and common rafters bear upon them at appropriate centres. The upper cruck is in many ways like the true cruck but for the blades rising from the first-floor collar or tie-beam. The wall plate may be connected to the cruck by means of the cruck spur or by means of a wrought-iron strap (see Fig 37).

The detail became common in smaller medieval houses built with a main structural frame a storey and a half high. In this instance the eaves-level tie-beam caused an obstruction in the upper storey. In such cases the smaller collar may be left out of the design, the cruck blades rising directly from the principal collar at lower level. In this detail the principal collar was morticed into the wall post which in turn was attached to the cruck blade by means of a cruck spur or iron

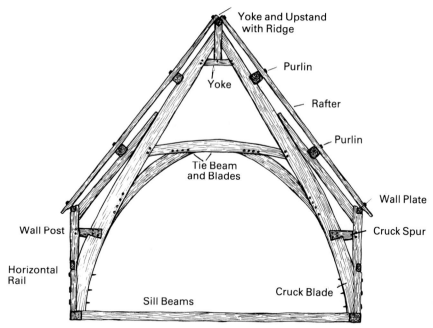

Fig 40 **Sixteenth-century cruck frame.** Note the yoke and upstand, ridge and curved braces to the lower tie-beam. Sill beams are also provided.

strap. The wall post exceeded the height of the top face of the principal collar and the wall plate was affixed to the top of the wall post. In this fashion the upper cruck blades were substantially inside the outer roof planes which were formed with common rafters spanning from wall plate to the roof ridge and bearing on an inter-mediatary purlin trenched into the cruck blade at a point close to the ridge (see Fig 40). The ridge type varies from building to building, but a yoke and upstand (see Figs 36a, c) or a variation of the tenoned upstand are relatively common. The upper cruck can be found in the Highland zone and some examples have been recorded in East Anglia.

In the south-west of England it is possible to see a further variation of the cruck frame, although strictly the structure has only the general appearance of a cruck. The 'jointed cruck' is formed of two timbers jointed together to form a frame which has a cruck-like appearance. The timbers are usually joined with a long mortice-and-tenoned joint which is cut so that the tenon is at the top of the wall post and the mortice in the inclined blade. The complete joint is exaggerated in length and pegged, often with several pegs for strength. This type of cruck is often called a 'scarf cruck' because, as

59

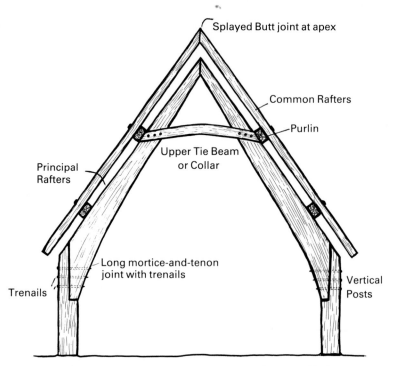

Splayed Butt joint at apex

Common Rafters

Purlin

Upper Tie Beam
or Collar

Principal
Rafters

Long mortice-and-tenon
joint with trenails

Trenails

Vertical
Posts

Fig 41 **Jointed cruck or scarf cruck.** In this structure the cruck blades are jointed at the point indicated. Purlins are provided. Common in the West and South West of England, the frame is not a true cruck.

an alternative to the tenon detail, it is sometimes found that the main structural timbers are cut into a splayed scarf joint (see Fig 41).

When this occurs, the joint is face pegged from the inside often with several pegs for rigidity. In the South West, timber-frame building was not so common as external walls were largely built of local stone. Internally, however, timber was used as a feature, and very often the jointed cruck formed the main roof structure and became a structural frame for elaborate plank and stud work in partition screens. The jointed cruck certainly has medieval origins. There are, however, more examples from the seventeenth and eighteenth centuries.

Cruck buildings varied in length from about one bay to three bays, the main internal space divided between the owner, his family and the byre containing animals. There might be a through passage connecting the areas for convenience. The living area was normally at the end furthest from the byre for obvious reasons; this in turn may have been divided to form a smaller enclosed room which was sometimes lofted over to provide separate sleeping accommodation.

The principal form of heat was an open fire, usually in the centre of the living area, so the room had to be full height to enable the smoke to escape through a roof hole. The room may have had primitive shuttered windows but must have been very cold and draughty in winter. Rain-water would also have freely penetrated the room through the smoke hole in the roof. In order to overcome this problem, small louvres may have been provided through which the smoke could escape. The early cruck, especially that belonging to a small family, was not built to a high standard and the scantlings used were of inferior size and quality. Needless to say, none of the original early crucks of this standard have survived, but there are better quality crucks of medieval origin in existence, mostly forming part of a larger and extended building.

The primitive cruck lasted for longer in the North and the West-country where standards were not so advanced; in the Highlands the basic form was still in existence well into the eighteenth century. The

Fig 42 **Yorkshire cruck and wall panel detail.** Note the extended main tie-beam and upper tie-beam or collar. These are framed into intermediate studs to form vertical wall panels. The sill beam is raised.

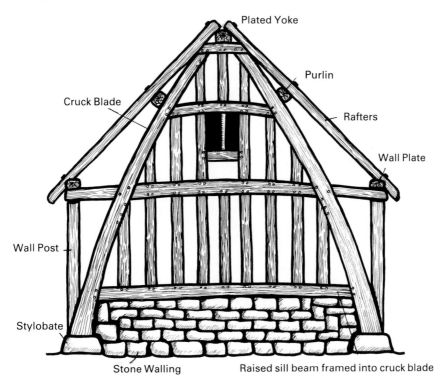

Plated Yoke

Purlin

Cruck Blade

Rafters

Wall Plate

Wall Post

Stylobate

Stone Walling

Raised sill beam framed into cruck blade

61

main disadvantage with cruck construction was that the span and overall height of the building were limited by the size of the cruck blades. It is true that the lower collars were often extended effectively to push out the roof span and overall width of the building, but such an extension was still limited and as a result the box-frame style of construction developed.

THE BOX FRAME

Why then did the inverted V-shaped structure of the Saxon house change? The answer was simply that it was not easy to expand an inverted V-shaped house in any direction but its length. The design also limited headroom over a substantial amount of the ground-floor space, and it became clear to the medieval carpenter that the wall and roof frames must be separate in order to make more space. The wall framing was set out on what was essentially a rectangular base of ground sills or sole plates. The usual detail was for the sills to be

Fig 43 **The box frame.** Box frame construction allows for the roof and wall frames to be independent of each other. Each section of frame is braced for stability. The frame is constructed on a bay system.

Two Bays

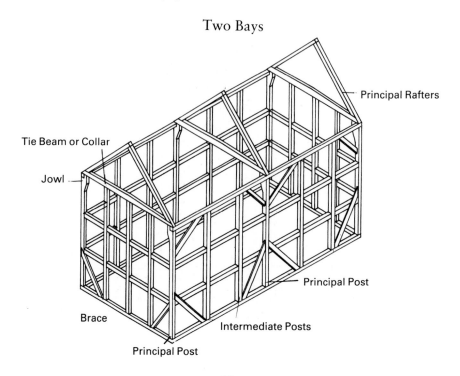

morticed at the corners where the huge timbers joined. To avoid the effects of rising damp, the timbers were usually set out or laid on low stone walls. When the timbers were laid on stone plinths, any imperfections in the shape of the wood or stonework were compensated for by means of wedges which corrected any irregularities when driven into the offending void. The wedges also, to an extent, enabled the sills to be levelled. The word used for this exercise was 'underpinning', and even today the word is common in building where structural irregularities occur in building foundations (see Plate 12).

The next stage was to erect the principal corner posts which were morticed into the sill corners and which carried the wall plates – the large horizontal timbers upon which the main loadings of the roof bear. The wall plates span between the corner posts and are effectively propped at set distances by the other vertical wall posts which make up the wall frame (see Fig 43 and Plates 12–17). Horizontal members were jointed into the sides of the vertical posts to give stiffening support. Wind braces of the tension and arch types gave

Fig 44 **Wattle and daub panel details.** Please see Appendix 2 for specification. (See Fig 64 for slate details.)

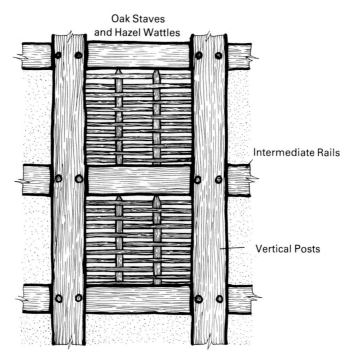

Oak Staves
and Hazel Wattles

Intermediate Rails

Vertical Posts

support to the vertical posts, horizontal plates and bressummers. Door and window openings were formed and the remaining panels were infilled, often with wattle and daub. This provided a lightweight and waterproof outer skin which was usually smoothed over on the surface and limewashed. (Further discussion of wall panels may be found on pp123–30.)

The traditional medieval timber frame was intended by the carpenter to be exposed both internally and externally. In East Anglia certain buildings break this general rule and were quite obviously intended by their builders to be plastered. As has been said, spaces formed by the principal and intermediate posts and sole plates needed to be filled, and many methods existed whereby this was achieved. By far the most common is wattle and daub, often known as 'stud and mud'. This type of panelling was common in most parts of the country and became an established method for weatherproofing framing timbers, which could then be reduced to the minimum required to support the roof loadings. The term is used to describe the method by which holes or slots of about 1in (2.5cm) in diameter were cut into the underside of the member forming the top of the panel. A groove was cut into the topside of the member forming the bottom of the panel (see Figs 44, 64 (pp63 and 96) and Plates 18–21). The medieval carpenter cut oak staves with the top shaped into a point and the bottoms cut into a chisel shape to fit the groove. The pointed end was inserted into the hole of the upper member and the stave forced into the opening, its bottom chisel cut and firmly wedged into the groove. The staves were commonly fixed at 1ft (30cm) to 1½ft (45cm) centres throughout the panel. The next stage was for the carpenter to cut lengths or strips of hazel or cleft oak which were interwoven in a basket-like fashion around the oak staves. The panel was then daubed on both sides with a mix of animal dung, chopped straw and clay. It was preferable to get the mix quite dry so that excessive shrinkage did not occur. The final finish might be a coat of thin plaster and limewash for waterproofing purposes.

The finished panel had extremely high weatherproofing qualities and examples have lasted for five hundred years. Correct and proper maintenance, however, is very necessary, but this is often neglected with disastrous results. The writer's own early fifteenth-century house had an extremely well-preserved flank wall, the upper portions of which were contained in the roof void. The house had a much later outshot with a cat-slide which dated from the late sixteenth century. Great excitement was felt when the wall was discovered for the first

Plate 18 (above left) **Wattle and framing members exposed.** The wattles are now ready to receive a mix of daub. See Appendix 2.

Plate 19 (above right) **Wattle and framing members.** Here different types of wattle are used. Note the difference.

Plate 20 (below left) **Wattle and daub.** A restored and limewashed wall panel with some weathering.

Plate 21 (below right) **Window detail.** Note the vertical window bars and limewashed elevations.

time; the surface limewash had dried to a dusty white where the structure had been hidden from the elements for so long. The cobwebs and dust were lightly brushed from the surface of the panelling and thereafter any visitors to the house were led not only through the main rooms and the cellar but, if they were energetic enough, into the roof to see our wall!

In East Anglia details were somewhat different in that the oak staves were set horizontally rather than vertically and the hazel wattles were not interwoven but tied to them. In a tall panel, where the width of the infill may not be any greater than the width of the vertical stud, there is clearly no room for the conventional vertical stave. The common detail in this instance is to set horizontally affixed staves across from stud to stud where they are wedged by means of a groove cut into the side of the stud. The oak staves are usually chisel ended as with vertically set panelling. The staves are set side by side to form a wall and are commonly finished off with a coat of plaster. In more northern areas, where stone is a better, available material and where close studding is common, the infill panels are often constructed from stone slabs laid and wedged between the studs in a similar manner to the oak staves (see Fig 64). Again, it is common for the stones to be plaster finished on both sides. In other areas, oak panelling is cut and wedged between the close studs, but this is not usually seen on external walls, although the writer has seen it used in this context. In the South East and Midlands, brick is a common infill panel material and would appear to have been used on early houses as an alternative to wattle and daub. The bricks are most commonly laid in a herring-bone pattern between close studding. In more open studding, the brickwork may be laid in different bands with herring-bone, a feature on certain main panels. The wattle-and-daub panel has been removed from many houses and brickwork used for infill instead. The main disadvantage of brick-work as infill is its poor insulation quality when used only in a single skin; bricks with lime mortar pointing also tend to hold dampness. These qualities can cause much in the way of discomfort to the householder. Bricks are also far heavier than wattle and daub and may stress the structural frame.

In order to combat the effects of dampness (see p68) many house-holders have rendered the external timber-framed, brick-infilled panels and thus covered over the essential framing of the structure. There are many interesting and beautiful timber frames hidden away all over the country because of this problem. Two or three years ago the writer helped to gut a house which had exterior walls in 9in (22.5cm) brickwork at the front and rear and was apparently part of a terrace of late Georgian and early Victorian houses. The previous owner of this property had spent hundreds of pounds in trying to proof the property against the effects of dampness, and he hoped to improve the insulation quality of the front and rear exterior walls. The gable walls were party walls with the adjoining cottages and heat loss was thus reduced, although he expended the same efforts to thicken out these walls as with the front and rear. His method was to nail 8 × 4ft (2.4 × 1.2m) hardboard panels over softwood timber studs which he nailed to the old wall coverings. These were largely wallpaper finishes over older panelling. Several generations of owners had all added their own finishes to the walls which included many layers of wallpaper, brown paper, newspaper and dress patterns cut up and methodically pasted to the walls! At the start of stripping out we discovered vertical and horizontal studs with infill panels of wattle and daub on the two gable or party wall ends. It took a weekend to strip a room approximately 12 × 12ft (3.6 × 3.6m) – at least, when we started, the room was that size. When we had filled a container skip to the brim with hardboard, rotted soft-wood, battens and studs and mouldy damp wallpaper, the room grew by more than 1ft (30cm) in either direction. We were left with the gable-end frames of a rather pleasing sixteenth-century cottage which still retained its original exterior wall panelling on the party walls, which were, of course, once visible from outside before the later Georgian and Victorian cottages were built. Unfortunately, as is so often the case, the Victorians had removed the ground-floor front and rear wall frames and built the structure up in 9in (22.5cm) brick-work to eaves' level. The first-floor wall frames were still in the building, although well hidden away in recesses formed in the brick-work. At the time of the Victorian alterations, a problem was encountered with first-floor joists which spanned from front to rear of the building via a trimmer mounted across the building from gable end to gable end. The joists were originally mortice and tenoned into a bressummer in the front-wall timber frame. When the frame was removed, the bressummer also disappeared and the joist ends were without any support; indeed, they stopped short of the new front-wall brickwork by some 12–14in (30–35cm). To overcome this problem the Victorian carpenter cut ends from other joists and simply nailed them to the existing joist ends, effectively increasing the length by about 1ft 6in (45cm). The new joist ends were then built into the 9in (22.5cm) wall and remain there today. The writer often looks at that detail and wonders why the entire first floor has not caved in. The purpose of telling this tale is that there are many other houses where such construction has been adopted, usually to hide the dampness in the original wall panels and perhaps attempt to insulate the walls at the same time. The defects and rectification techniques covered in the restoration pages of this book may well be of interest to those readers with similar problems.

CLADDINGS

Other means of keeping out dampness vary somewhat from area to area. From the end of the sixteenth century, in particular, many older timber-framed houses were clad mainly to provide weather- and draught-proof walls. The most common was external plastering which was probably also the oldest method. Plastering became

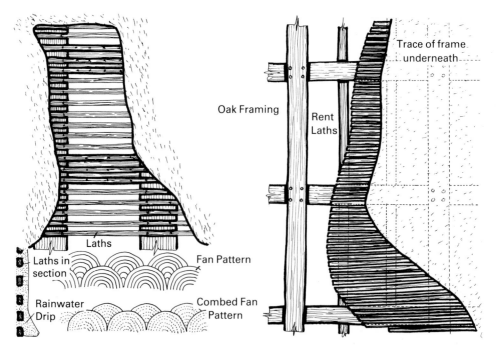

Fig 45 **Plaster claddings.** Plaster is applied to riven timber laths as shown. Usually two coats are applied to the outside wall face. The frame shown has heavy oak vertical and horizontal members and is typical of the Eastern School.

Fig 46 **Plaster and pargetting.** Plaster is applied to rent laths which are in turn nailed to the structural frame. Typical patterns are shown in Fig 45.

extremely popular in the seventeenth century and gained in popularity during the eighteenth century. It was easier to get softwood laths and the quality of plaster improved quite considerably. It was common to leave the original wattle-and-daub panelling intact and to cover only the external face with closely spaced riven laths which were usually nailed to the external face of the oak studs. The laths were then plastered over externally to form a new outer wall covering. The inside walls were left in their original form with all oak studs and horizontal members exposed. Sometimes the original wattle-and-daub panelling was removed. This may have been because it was considered defective or beyond repair. Where this occurred, the timber laths forming the key for new plasterwork were nailed to both exterior and interior faces of the frame and the whole structure was plastered. In the south-east of England plaster cladding was considered a feature and as a result became the most popular method of weatherproofing (see Figs 45–6).

During the sixteenth and seventeenth centuries, many new houses were constructed so that the timber frames, formerly meant to adorn the property, were hidden. Because the frames were designed to be hidden, the joinery details were often less than good and the quality of the timber was often second-rate. Many such houses have now suffered the latest fashion whereby such timber frames are stripped of plaster and nailed laths to expose timbers never intended for display. Many such timbers are stained with rust from the old nails and horizontal strips on the wood can be clearly seen where the laths have been removed. The trend today is to stain and treat the wood with one of the proprietary brands of preservative, but the end result is less than satisfactory and is certainly not traditional.

Plaster claddings, together with wattle-and-daub infilling, are able to offer a measure of protection to the period timber-framed house. It is, however, necessary to protect the outside surface of the cladding material against the natural effects of weathering and the method most adopted for doing this was limewashing. While this was the traditional method and, as mentioned earlier, may have been one reason why period timber-framed houses were often referred to as 'black and white', the limewash was in reality porous and would have needed refreshing perhaps every year. It is more likely that it was left for two years or more and then the oak frame as well as the wattle-and-daub panel would have been limewashed. The reason for this is that rain-water could trickle into the joints between the panel and the frame and thus penetrate the building, destroying internal finishes and causing discomfort to the occupier. The limewash would effectively penetrate the joints and seal them up, thus making it more difficult for water to penetrate. Because of these problems, other methods of cladding were adopted, and it is possible that the most attractive detail of jettying originated out of the desire to throw surface water away from the walls, especially at low level.

In the south-east of England, a 'prentice' board was one method adopted to keep water away from the exterior walls. The prentice board is a timber board affixed to the face of the wall usually on timber brackets. The board is set at an angle in such a way as to throw the surface water away from the wall and is more often than not attached to the gable ends of the building. In the west Midlands it was common to affix a small area of roof at ground- and first-floor ceiling levels outside the building. The roof was normally tiled and acted in the same way as the prentice board in throwing water away from the building. This was often adopted in conjunction with wattle-and-daub panelling, but in buildings where the wattle and daub has been replaced with other material, such as brick, it has unfortunately disappeared.

Wattle and daub together with plaster is sometimes called 'stud and mud' (see Glossary of Terms). The specification, which varies in different parts of the country, might suggest a sand-to-lime ratio of one to two, giving a suitably sticky bonding agent for the hair and straw reinforcing. In other areas, four parts of white lime putty might be mixed with one part of sharp sand and one part of cow dung (see Appendix 2). In some areas, the plaster was worked and decorated, this ornamentation being called pargeting. The incised type of pargeting was sometimes known as 'stick work' because of the crudity of the basic tools used to gain the effect; a pointed stick or a comb would be used to cut a design into the wet plaster. Raised pargeting, more common in the late seventeenth and early eighteenth centuries, required more skill and the design was put on to the wet plaster in relief form.

A very common method of weatherproofing is by means of tile-hanging, and there are many thousands of timber-framed houses throughout the country where this had been adopted. The early examples of original tile-hanging date from the seventeenth century when the basic idea of covering both frame and panel was conceived. During this period there was a shortage of good structural timber, especially in the South, so beams tended to be second-rate and there-fore appropriate for covering over. At first plain tiles were used, laid

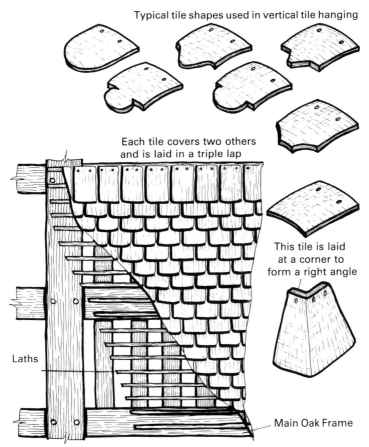

Typical tile shapes used in vertical tile hanging

Each tile covers two others
and is laid in a triple lap

This tile is laid
at a corner to
form a right angle

Laths

Main Oak Frame

Fig 47 **Tile hanging.** Typical tile hanging to a heavy timber-framed wall. Each tile has a triple lap and each covers two others.

in a triple lap and hung on horizontally fixed softwood battens nailed to the oak studs. A triple lap meant that each tile lapped two others, as shown in the illustration (Fig 47.) To overcome the problem of corners and jambs, special tiles were manufactured as shown in the illustration. An alternative method of fixing tiles, although used more on brick than timber-framed houses, was to nail the tile into the horizontal mortar joints. The writer has seen this detail when a wattle-and-daub panel, ironically with relatively good insulation qualities, was removed and replaced by a brick panel with poorer insulation qualities. The brick panel was then clad in tile-hanging nailed to the mortar courses and occasionally the oak studs (see Plates 21a–b).

It is now a common sight to see decorated tile-hanging of the fish-

71

Plate 21a **Wattle and daub.** The limewash coverings are weathered and the wattle and daub exposed beneath.
Plate 21b **Wall panels.** An example of recent brick infill panel to an early timber-framed house.

scale and hammer-head patterns (see Fig 47). While tiling of this type can often be seen on period timber-framed houses of considerable age, the tiling is almost certainly only Victorian or newer. Tile-hanging is most likely to be found in Surrey and Kent and is very common in Sussex, particularly the Weald where the original red clays adorn the landscape. Kentish tiles are constructed with an irregular shape and a slightly curved face, but are otherwise plain in appearance. The tiles of Surrey tend to be more decorated than plain. Tiles were an established material in London, mainly as a precaution against fire – witness the Great Fire of London in 1666. During the seventeenth century they were used more in the South East, although they were restricted to the upper walls and gable ends which were more exposed than the lower structure.

A development of earlier tile-hanging was the 'mathematical' tile, hung or nailed to horizontally fixed softwood battens or boarding. The tile was cleverly designed with a brick-shaped squared end which resembled the face of a brick. The hidden part of the tile had a tapered face and was nailed through to the batten or board. The tiles were laid in stretcher-bond pattern and corners were usually achieved with purpose-made tiles. To complete the illusion of brickwork, the horizontal and perpendicular joints were pointed up in mortar. The mathematical tile was adopted in Sussex and Kent but mainly in the towns.

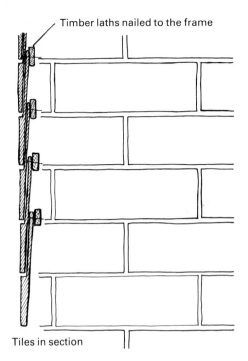

Timber laths nailed to the frame

Tiles in section

Fig 48 **Mathematical tiling in elevation.** When properly hung these tiles have the appearance of a brick wall.

An experience has been described in a friend's cottage where the original timber-framed front and rear walls were removed during the Victorian period and replaced in 9in (22.5cm) brickwork. We know that this work took place during the nineteenth century because it is well recorded and at the time several other buildings in the same street underwent major structural alterations. The process of replacing timber frame with brick was popularised during the seventeenth and eighteenth centuries when the production of bricks was stepped up to meet the ever-increasing demand. There may have been a practical logic for this exercise, as well as a desire to comply with fashion. The writer has surveyed many houses in which the walls on all principal elevations have undergone extensive structural alteration. It would seem plausible that in many cases the original timber frame had rotted or decayed to such an extent that it became unsteady and required some form of underpinning. The fashion of brickwork allowed the frame to be underpinned at a suitable point, and it would seem that the most convenient point was at first-floor level, either below or in the immediate proximity of the bressummers carrying the first-floor wall frames and structural loadings. The writer's own early fifteenth-century house had unfortunately undergone such treatment in the late seventeenth century and the principal

Plate 22 **Wall panels.** An example of timber cladding to a fifteenth-century building, in Surrey.
Plate 23 **Wall panels.** The Wealden house at the Weald and Downland Open Air Museum at Singleton, Sussex.

posts were sawn off just below the mortice-and-tenon joint created for the bressummers. The entire structure was underpinned with brickwork on the front and gable elevations but had been allowed to stand on the rear elevation because of the outshot constructed as an extension to the original frame. It was also common during the sixteenth and seventeenth centuries to clad a timber-framed house in brick, thus hiding the 'old-fashioned' wattle-and-daub panels. The writer has looked at houses treated in this way in Sussex, Kent and Surrey and has knowledge of others in the Westcountry.

The object of cladding a period timber-framed house was to keep out the weather and increase the comfort of the owner; fashion and availability of materials also played an important part in the method by which a timber-framed house might be clad. Financial restrictions often prevented a small cottage or house being clad in any of the more suitable materials already described. One of the cheapest and simplest methods of cladding was clapboarding or weather-boarding which, in its early days, was often formed in oak or elm pegged to the principal posts and studs of the timber frame. We know it was in use at the start of the seventeenth century, mainly on rural buildings such as barns and other similar constructions, but it did not develop on domestic buildings until the start of the eighteenth century. Later examples of weather-boarding are in softwood and the methods of fixing are shown in Plate 22.

74

2 ROOFS

The process of actually dating a house can be confused by later alterations to the basic structure which have affected the outer walls and reshaped the roof. It could be said that the roof of a building is as good as the contents page of a book in setting out the development of the building over the years. Structural and heavy cosmetic changes to a building are most likely to affect the outer walls. Extensions to a roof might well appear obvious immediately after completion because of the clear newness of the structural elements used, but after a century or two the natural ageing process obscures the facts, and the constant development and alteration process common to all buildings only helps to compound the situation.

In timber-framed buildings there is usually a clear relationship between the plan form of a building and the bay system adopted at the time. For instance, one bay consisting of one room was common. Things are, however, never so easy and the provision of a cross-frame might allow a room to be open on one floor and closed on another. In this way a ground floor may be divided into two single-bay rooms, but on the floor above the area may consist of a double-bay room not subdivided.

Other intermediate roof trusses could also be added, each dividing the structural bay length accordingly. The medieval open hall often consisted of two bays with a central, open-arched, cross-framed roof truss. It could be said that timber-frame building reached a climax in the construction of the open hall where the attention to internal detail was something to be admired. It is still possible to discover tell-tale soot marks of the open hall on the aged timbers of a farmhouse attic, since altered to such an extent that the original structure is completely hidden or disguised. In the latter part of the sixteenth century, the open hall became less popular and as a result the style and subsequent constructional details died.

The principle of the open hall was the creation of a large open space, usually to the roof, and centred around an open fire burning on a hearth. In a poorer house, the principle was the same and the space provided was meant for the family and all their worldly belongings. As discussed earlier, only the better quality buildings have survived and it follows therefore that evidence of the low-quality, open-hall style is archaeological, derived from the remains discovered on known medieval village sites. Features of the open hall are common in surviving buildings, although there are regional differences. The concept of the hall was to provide a well-organised and open space set out and arranged in such a way that each separate element had its own individuality and formal purpose. One end of the hall would be reserved for the owner and his family and some provision was made for their privacy. This end of the building was commonly known as the 'solar' and formed in effect a private apartment.

At the solar end of the hall it was usual to have the high table which in some cases may have been mounted on a dais to emphasise the importance of the owner. In addition to the dais, and especially if the owner was a lord or nobleman, there may have been decoration to the surrounding timberwork. Often the tie-beam immediately behind the high table was heavily moulded. Any important house guest or visitor would be seated on trestles near the high table, and the food, which was normally cooked outside, was brought into the building for consumption. In the centre of the hall would be the open hearth; smoke was allowed to escape from the building via large planked doors, the thatched roof and in some cases tall windows called 'wind holes' which were often situated in close proximity to the owner's high table. The wind holes were not protected against the elements and a considerable amount of rain and snow must have freely penetrated the building during inclement weather.

On entering the hall from the usual entrance passage, the fire was probably the first thing seen by a visitor to a building. The hall was usually separated from the pantry and the buttery by means of tall screens between which the entrance passage led to the open hall and to the outside. The buttery and pantry doors were often opposite the main door to the open hall. In addition to the main structure, the open hall may have had wings added at either or both ends, and in some buildings the solar chamber may have been contained at first-floor level. The owner's animals, which would have included oxen and horses, were more than likely brought in at night for protection and security.

The open-hall roof was formed with a massive central open truss allowing for the provision of two bays, each being approximately 15ft (4.5m) in length, although this may vary from region to region (see Plates 22 and 23). The constructional details of the open-hall roof vary from region to region, but the principal collar or tie-beam is braced where the principal rafters bear on to the external structural wall posts (see Fig 50). This arrangement always occurs, unless a cruck frame has been adopted, in which case there is often a collar approximately midway between ground level and the apex of the cruck. The principle of this is to form a structural A-frame and thus avoid the effects of roof spread around the cruck blades. The central open truss is not always centrally spaced in the building, and

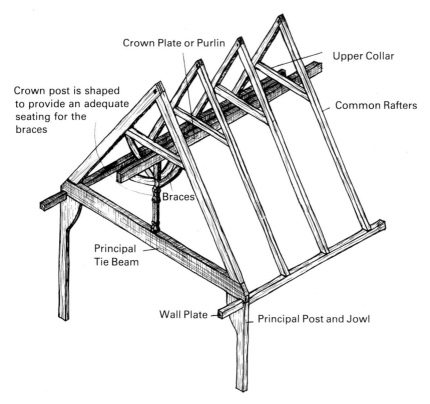

Fig 49 **Crown post roof. Typical roof truss.** This is a classic double rafter roof. The crown post rises from the centre of a principal tie-beam and carries the crown plate or crown purlin. This supports the upper collars jointed to each set of rafters. The collar purlin is braced back to the crown post for stability as shown.

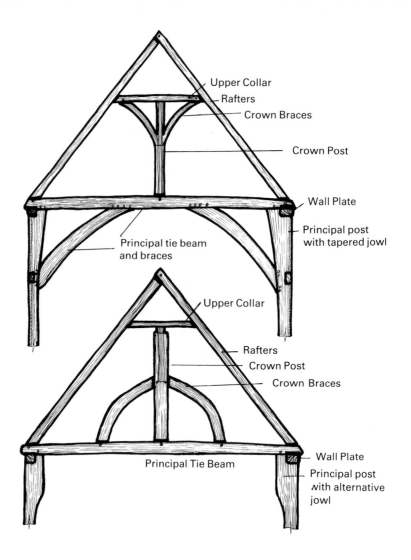

Fig 50 **Open hall roof details.** Typical variations of crown post construction.

the bay size on either side might vary by as much as 2–3ft (60–90cm) overall. The crown-post roof is one of the most attractive types of truss roof and is commonly found in open-hall roof construction (see Figs 49–51 and Plates 24–6). In this detail a short post rises from the centre of the principal collar or tie-beam and carries a horizontal purlin or plate, which in turn supports the smaller collar used to tie the common rafters together. The collar purlin was usually braced back to the crown post, and in some cases extra struts were provided

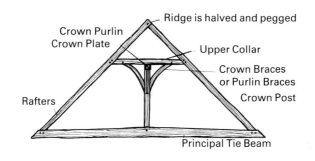

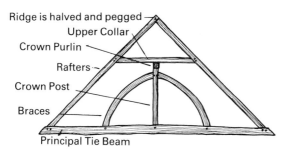

Fig 51 **Crown post details.** Note the variations in bracing style to the crown post.

from the crown post to the smaller collar. The crown-post roof was more predominant in the South East and in East Anglia, although they do appear in other areas, nearly always in high quality medieval buildings situated in important towns.

Some very early crown posts are known, but generally they would appear to have been developed from an earlier, simpler form of roof construction in which there were no longitudinal timbers and each pair of rafters was joined by a collar and braced by means of battening which was attached directly to the outer roof covering. The earlier design had obvious weaknesses in that the entire and completed roof was not adequately braced. The failure of one set of rafters could cause it to fall against the next, and so collapse like a pack of cards, which must have happened many times in early roof construction.

The crown post was thus introduced to overcome this potentially destructive problem in roof construction, and, together with the collar purlin or crown plate, a successful method of lateral restraint was conceived. The collar purlin had the effect of restraining the

Plate 24 **Crown post roofs.** This crown post roof is in the process of complete restoration. Note the size of timbers used.

Plate 25 (right) **Crown post roofs.** A crown post roof in the early stages of construction prior to being added to the main building. Plate 26 (below) **Crown post roofs.**

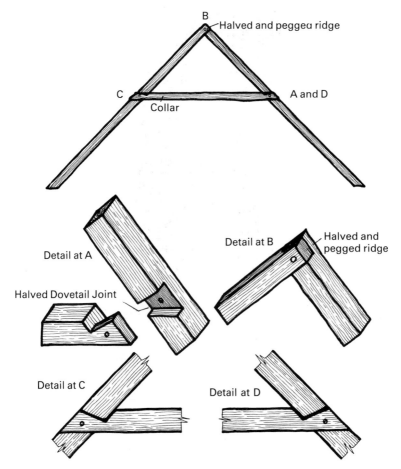

B
Halved and pegged ridge

C
A and D
Collar

Detail at A

Detail at B
Halved and pegged ridge

Halved Dovetail Joint

Detail at C

Detail at D

Fig 52 **Single collar rafter roof.** Each pair of rafters is triangulated separately but no ridge or purlin is provided.

rafters and transferred substantial roof loadings to the main tie-beams via the crown post. The crown posts were set at even intervals along the building frame and were fixed via the decorated bases into principal tie-beams and via the decorated caps into the underside of the collar purlin, or crown plate as it is sometimes known.

The crown posts were braced with the collars and the collar purlin in order to prevent lateral movement and subsequent collapse. In three main types of truss design, the main variable is the method by which the crown post is linked to the crown plate or collar purlin and how it is braced. In a typical truss, on which the crown post is braced to the collar purlin, the following may apply.

The base of the short post is tenoned to the top face of the main

81

collar beam which spans the building from side to side. At a point approximately two-thirds towards the top of the triangular section formed by the principal rafters and the main collar, a further collar or tie of a smaller section scantling is provided, and this sits on the crown plate or collar purlin for support. The lateral braces vary in form from this point (see Fig 51).

In some instances it will be seen that the braces are joined to the post to form a crown-like appearance, with the braces mortice-and-tenon jointed into the four sides of the post and then connected into the underside of the collar purlin and the secondary rafter tie-beam (see Figs 49–51). When the cap and base plates are decorated, which is often the case, this is a wonderful piece of joinery. Such a detail was common in the fifteenth century and examples still exist in Kent. A derivation of this method of bracing is to connect only the collar purlin to the crown post by means of mortice-and-tenoned braces and to leave the secondary upper tie-beam unconnected.

A third method of achieving lateral support is by the connection of the crown-post cap to the underside of the collar purlin. The secondary tie-beam then bears directly on to the collar purlin and thus the crown post. The essential difference in this variation is the method of supporting the crown post which, instead of bracing against the collar purlin and the secondary tie-beam, is braced against the upper face of the principal collar. The braces form an arched structure connected to the principal collar and crown post by the provision of mortice-and-tenon joints. The position of the upper or secondary tie-beam may vary from region to region and, as already stated, is usually two-thirds the height of the triangular section formed by the principal rafters or truss. There are, however, instances when the secondary collar or tie-beam is situated at a point approximately midway along the truss section. It therefore follows that bracing at this point is likely to be less satisfactory, as more of a section is left unbraced. Because of this, a roof section employing a centrally placed collar is usually of lesser height.

The structural method by which the principal collar or tie-beam, wall post and wall plate are connected is common throughout the country, allowing for slight variations in style. The joint used, the tie-beam lap-dovetail joint, apart from being one of the most important joints, is also one of the most beautiful (see Fig 23, page 30). This joint connects the tie-beam to the wall plate, although a bare-faced joint is sometimes used, being one in which the shoulder is to one side only. In some cases the lap-dovetail joint opened up because of strain

82

and so created a gap. To overcome this defect, the shoulder of the joint was sometimes housed or entrant to increase stability (see Glossary of Terms and Fig 23). For a satisfactory joint, the maximum amount of timber was required to achieve sufficient rigidity. The wall post was commonly thickened out in a 'jowl', which was the root end of the original tree from which the post was cut. There are many variations of the jowl and these include flared, splayed, round, tapered, tapered with curved returns and tapered with square-cut returns (see Figs 25–9, pages 32–3).

The jowl was first used in the thirteenth century in a crude and basically undecorated form. During the sixteenth and seventeenth centuries it became highly decorated but lost much of its structural strength as a result. During the seventeenth and eighteenth centuries a long swelling jowl was used, but the detail was generally abandoned during the latter end of the eighteenth century.

We have said that the tie-beam lap-dovetail joint was common in the connection of wall post, principal collar and wall plates. There were, however, other joints used to connect the wall-post head to the collar beam and wall plate. In the thirteenth century a detail existed whereby the wall post was cut so that its upper edge had an unrefined tenon. The plate was cut with a square mortice into which the tenon on the post was placed. The collar ends were cut to form a square-set notched lap and the entire joint was thus pegged into place.

It was discovered that the assembled joint was weak, especially if any of the three constituent timbers rotted in the vicinity of the joint. Such a weakness ultimately caused the collapse of the joint and thus the structure of which it formed a part. A slightly later tying joint is illustrated and this shows an unrefined tenon on the wall post end with the front upstanding. The upstand stub is tenoned into the soffit of the tie-beam. The lap joint is of a lap-dovetail type with entrant shoulders and the tail is stopped short. The upstand is the probable origin of the jowl previously described. In the seventeenth century the joint developed with a cut jowl and a full lap-dovetail. The jowl tenon is sometimes called a 'teazle' tenon and was set to one side to avoid weakening the tail (see Fig 24, page 31).

Buildings dated between about 1380 and 1500 sometimes contained a joint which constituted a pair of single tenons placed on either side of the tail. This was better than the previous joint and conforms to the Tudor style. A joint commonly used during the fourteenth century was of a reversed assembly type where the jowl was rotated through 90°. This ingenious method, which created extra strength in the joint, was common in Essex after the start of the fifteenth century.

After the early part of the sixteenth century, the open hall was abandoned and roof timbers were no longer decorated. With the decorative function removed, it became more desirable to utilise roof space, which spawned the idea of the attic to gain valuable extra space. The crown post with the collar purlin proved to be a nuisance and a waste of space. As a direct result the side purlin roof came into its own because it gave the maximum amount of free space in the attic. In the South East the crown-post roof was replaced by the clasp purlin and the butt purlin. In more northern parts the clasp purlin was used but this was essentially a cruck-frame area and the clasp purlin was soon replaced by the heavy principal rafter roof.

CLASPED-PURLIN ROOF CONSTRUCTION

The principle of the clasped purlin can be seen in some of the earliest surviving roofs, and examples were built throughout the whole medieval period, even when the crown-post roof was predominant. After c1500 the clasped purlin became almost the standard construction and lasted in parts of England until the nineteenth century (see Fig 53). In this form of construction the principal rafters are mortice and tenoned into the principal collar and bear upon the wall post. The upper ends of the wall post often have a jowl and the wall plate is jointed into the jowl in order that the outside edge of the plate is on the same plane as the outside edge of the wall post.

The characteristics of the clasped-purlin roof are that the principal rafters are cut with their upper face in line with the common rafters. The upper portion of the principal rafter is cut to a smaller section than the lower portion, and the collar mortice is cut immediately below the point at which the rafter changes in size. The purlin is clasped in the cut-out portion by the end of the collar which is notched to hold the purlin in position. The joint between the collar and principal rafter is commonly a mortice-and-tenon type. The collar is further held in place by means of a strut. This is mortice and tenoned into the top face of the principal collar at above plate level and the underside of the top collar being that which clasps the purlin. Two such struts are normally provided.

A variation of this calls for the use of a curved strut which is cut to clasp the purlin and which has a tenon on its upper edge, this being connected to the underface of the principal rafter and pegged. The

84

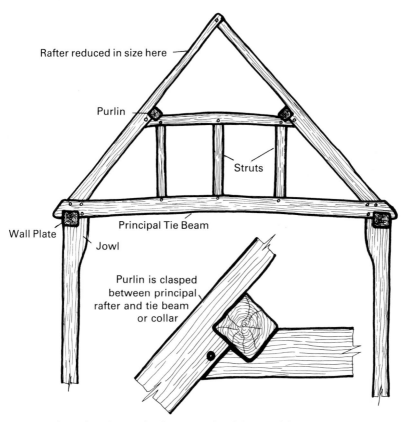

Labels in figure:
Rafter reduced in size here
Purlin
Struts
Wall Plate
Principal Tie Beam
Jowl
Purlin is clasped between principal rafter and tie beam or collar

Fig 53 **Clasped purlin roof.** The principle of this roof form can be seen in some of the earliest surviving roofs. After 1500 the clasped purlin roof became standard construction. It lasted until about the nineteenth century. The detail shows enlarged view of structure around purlin.

lower end is mortice and tenoned into the top edge of the principal collar in the usual manner. This variation of the clasped purlin eliminates the need for an upper collar or tie-beam.

TENONED OR BUTT-PURLIN ROOF CONSTRUCTION

This detail can be found in many parts of southern England and is commonly used as an alternative to the clasped purlin (see Figs 54 and 55). In some areas the detail is regarded as a feature of high quality medieval carpentry and generally the joint has good structural characteristics. The principal timbers needed are mainly of heavy section and comprise the following: wall post, often with a dowel insert, a pair of principal rafters of similar proportion in the

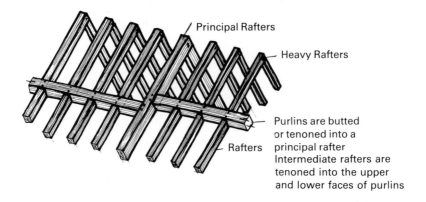

Principal Rafters

Heavy Rafters

Purlins are butted
or tenoned into a
principal rafter
Intermediate rafters are
tenoned into the upper
and lower faces of purlins

Rafters

Fig 54 **Tenoned or butt purlin (staggered).** This construction can be found in many parts of southern England. It is commonly used as an alternative to the clasp purlin and in certain areas regarded as a feature of high quality construction. See Fig 55.

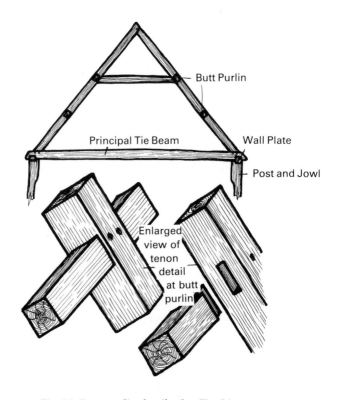

Butt Purlin

Principal Tie Beam

Wall Plate

Post and Jowl

Enlarged
view of
tenon
detail
at butt
purlin

Fig 55 **Butt purlin details.** See Fig 54.

upper and lower sections, and a plate jointed into the jowl of the wall post in a manner similar to that of the clasped purlin. The upper tie or collar is often of heavy section, too, and is mortice and tenoned into the inner face of the principal rafters at a point about two-thirds along the rafters at high level.

It is also common for the principal rafters to be strutted to the principal collar at a point just less than half-way along the length of the rafter. There are two main ways of connecting the purlins to the principal rafter, either directly in line or staggered. The in-line arrangement calls for a mortice to be cut in the sides of the principal rafter at a point very near the inside edge of the timber. Peg-holes are also provided for the completion of the joint. The ends of the purlins are cut into tenons and these are inserted into the morticed sides of the principal rafters. The same principle applies when the purlins are staggered, but the mortices are cut out of line so that the purlins, when connected, do not line up on either side of the principal rafters. In this detail the common rafters may also be mortice and tenoned into the top and bottom faces of the purlin.

THROUGH- OR TRENCHED-PURLIN CONSTRUCTION

This detail, which may be derived from the cruck frame, is commonly found in areas where the cruck developed, the North, following the decline of the king post, and the West and Midlands, following the decline of cruck construction in the sixteenth century in those areas. In through-purlin construction the principal rafters are of somewhat larger section than the common rafters. They are mortice and tenoned into the ends of the principal tie-beam or collar, which in turn is connected to the wall plate and wall post. An upper collar is provided which may be connected to the principal collar by one or two struts which are mortice and tenoned into the lower face of the upper collar and upper face of the lower collar respectively (see Figs 56–7).

The purlins are trenched into the outer face of the main principal rafters which also commonly have a bird's mouth joint at the ridge to carry a ridge piece. This arrangement is rarely seen in the clasped- and butt-purlin roofs found in the South East. The common rafters are notched over the wall plate, bearing directly on to the trenched purlin, and when assembled are not on the same plane as the principal rafters. At the upper end they bear on to the ridge piece which is jointed with the mortice-and-tenoned ends of the principal rafters. In the fourteenth century the lower collar was often arched

87

and may have been decorated with arched braces back to the wall post. The inside edge of the principal rafters was sometimes elaborate, as were the struts lending support to the upper collar and principal rafters. It should be noted that this style of roof did not always include a ridge piece, although this was common from the fifteenth century onwards. The later wall posts also commonly had jowls on the upper ends, the style dependent upon the region and the carpenter (see Figs 56–7).

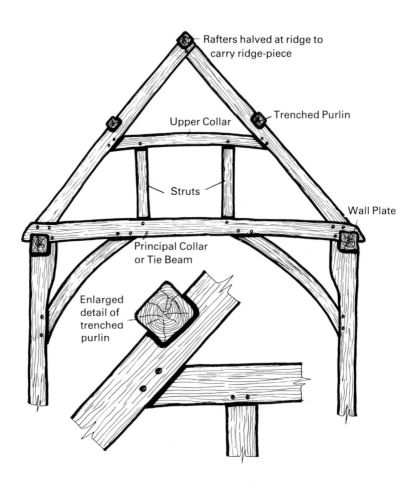

Fig 56 **Trenched purlin roof.** Also called a through purlin construction, trenched purlins may have derived from the cruck frame. This roof form is found in the North of England where crucks are also common.

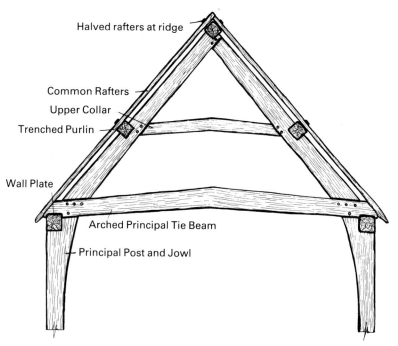

Halved rafters at ridge

Common Rafters

Upper Collar

Trenched Purlin

Wall Plate

Arched Principal Tie Beam

Principal Post and Jowl

Fig 57 **Truss with trenched or through purlins.** See Fig 56 for detail of trenched purlins.

ARCH-BRACED COLLAR BEAM CONSTRUCTION

Some medieval buildings, usually of better quality, were constructed with a first floor which often had a full storey height when the need for clear open space was important (see Fig 58). Other forms of truss had the effect of limiting passage from one bay to the next, but the provision of the arch-braced collar beam overcame this problem by discarding the main tie-beam and providing a collar at high level, usually at a point half-way up the length of the principal rafters. The collar was supported with arch braces, tenon jointed into the under-side of the principal rafters and the underside of the collar. Two further arch braces were tenoned into the top face of the collar, joining the underside of the principal rafters at a point just under half-way between the top of the collar and the inside apex of the ridge. The collar truss and wind braces were sometimes elaborately decorated. The bases of the principal rafters were notched over the wall plate; a main wall post was not provided. This type of construc-tion could only be used where side purlins were adopted and was most common where it formed an intermediate truss between other principal trusses (see Fig 58).

89

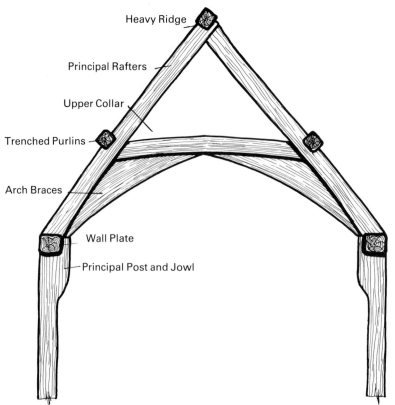

Heavy Ridge

Principal Rafters

Upper Collar

Trenched Purlins

Arch Braces

Wall Plate

Principal Post and Jowl

Fig 58 **Western style arch-braced collar beam roof.** This construction overcame the problem of constructional timber in upper floor areas and provided an interesting feature.

KING POST CONSTRUCTION

The king post is typical in the northern part of the country where all the rules of timber-frame building style are seemingly broken. Elsewhere this design was virtually unknown until the seventeenth century by which time it had proved itself as structurally sound.

In the North the detail was common in medieval halls where the construction was good, solid and plain, usually lacking in any form of decoration. Often the halls were aisled with walls formed of close-studded framing. The main posts often rested on stylobates, and the sills were tenoned into them in the interrupted style (see Fig 9, page 21, and Glossary of Terms). The king post is a stout post rising from the principal tie-beam to carry the ridge piece loadings. The principal rafters rise from the tie-beams and are tenoned into the side of the king post. The purlins are usually of smaller scantling and they are

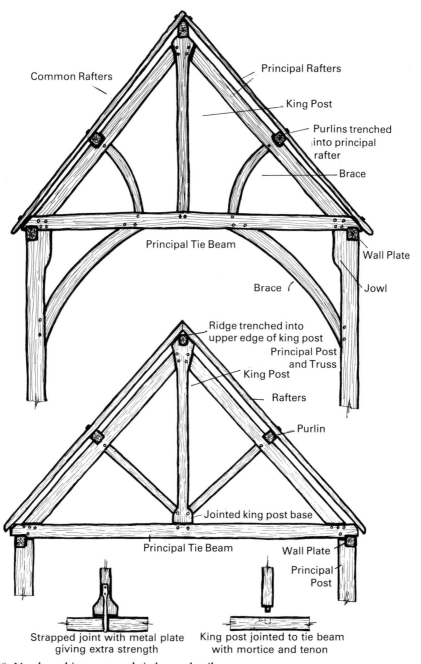

Fig 59 **Northern king post and tie beam detail.**
Fig 60 **King post roof construction.** This construction is typical of the North country. In other areas the detail is virtually unknown until the seventeenth century. Detail shows alternative methods of joining king posts to principal tie-beam.

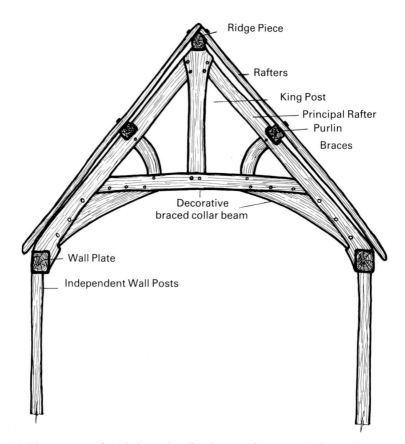

Ridge Piece

Rafters

King Post

Principal Rafter

Purlin

Braces

Decorative
braced collar beam

Wall Plate

Independent Wall Posts

Fig 61 **King post roof with braced collar beam.** This example has a decorative braced collar beam.

trenched into the sides of the principal rafters. The common rafters then bear directly upon the trenched purlins and the ridge. The top of the king post is usually shaped to allow bearing of the common rafters at the ridge. Sometimes the principal rafters were given additional support from struts bearing off the tie-beam (see Figs 60–1).

QUEEN POST CONSTRUCTION

It is still a mystery as to why the king post became popular in southern parts of the country during the eighteenth century. Coincident with that development was the way in which the queen posts, familiar in medieval buildings in Suffolk, took a different form in the eighteenth and nineteenth centuries (see Figs 62–3). The structure

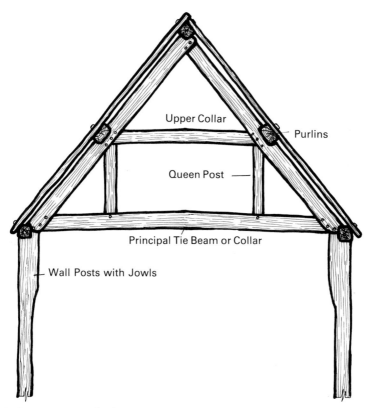

Fig 62 **Queen post roof.** The queen post developed coincident with the king post. It was familiar in medieval buildings of Suffolk but changed form in the eighteenth and nineteenth centuries. In their original form they appeared as a derivation of the aisled structure but posts were supported on the principal tie-beam rather than the ground.

was formed of a principal collar connected to wall posts and the wall plate in the usual manner. In their original form in Suffolk they appeared as a derivation of the aisled structure, but the posts were supported on the principal tie-beam rather than the ground.

The queen posts effectively propped the purlins and were cut with a bird's mouth joint on the upper edge for this purpose. It was common for the queen post roof to have two pairs of purlins. The lower pair were commonly trenched into the principal rafters and bore directly over two struts which were in turn tenoned into the bases of the queen posts on the outside edge. At a level just below the upper purlin, an upper collar or tie-beam was provided which was tenoned into the inside of the queen posts at the top. The structure was completed by a further post which was tenoned into the centre of

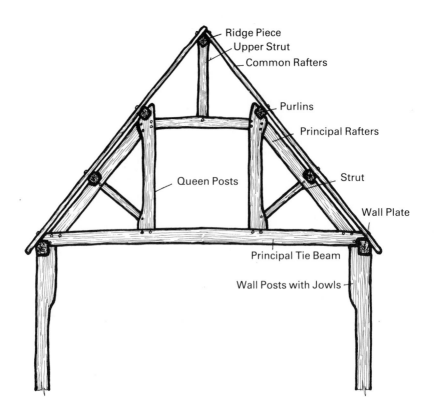

Ridge Piece
Upper Strut
Common Rafters
Purlins
Principal Rafters
Queen Posts
Strut
Wall Plate
Principal Tie Beam
Wall Posts with Jowls

Fig 63 **Alternative queen post roof.** In this example the queen posts prop the purlins.

the upper tie-beam. This was cut on its upper edge into a bird's mouth joint to carry the ridge piece and upper ridge loadings. The common rafters were laid over the trenched purlins and bore upon the ridge piece at the top and the edge of the main collar and plate at the bottom.

The eighteenth- and nineteenth-century examples of queen posts are similar to king posts in that they support the purlins and are jointed by a collar. The joint between the queen posts is sometimes enlarged or replaced by a strap on later examples. There are many examples of the queen post with interrupted tie-beams.

3 RESTORATION AND REPAIR WORK

Timber-framed buildings can be divided into two main types: the Tudor, with separate storeys, close studding and upper floors constructed with jetty details; and the later fully framed building with wide-braced panels and tall posts. The principle of the timber frame is that the structural loadings of the building are taken up by the frame while actual wall panels are non-structural. Panels, which may be formed of timber, wattle, brick or stone, are a cladding only to keep out the elements. It is therefore essential to understand fully the mechanics of the timber frame and the way in which the principal timbers are set and braced and the design of the bays. In dealing with a period timber-framed house, it will be found that many alterations have been made, not necessarily with due regard for these essential factors, and, as a result of the alterations, settlement and structural distortion in the building frame may well have occurred.

It is absolutely essential to make a detailed examination of the building to be restored before making any effort to open up and uncover any hidden structure which is believed to be present: by carrying out both a structural and measured survey of the building, the details of construction methods will be revealed. It will be found that once the building plan is drawn in black and white, the true extent of original building will become more obvious. The structural survey will draw attention to the overall thickness of walls, the relationship of walls and inside floor levels to outside ground levels, and it will give evidence of hidden ground sills and whether the ground-floor wall framing has been removed in part or in whole, as is common in many areas. The main structural wall posts will be highlighted, as will the principal trusses in the roof void.

From this information it can be seen how the building developed and how many bays it had in its original form. As said earlier, the

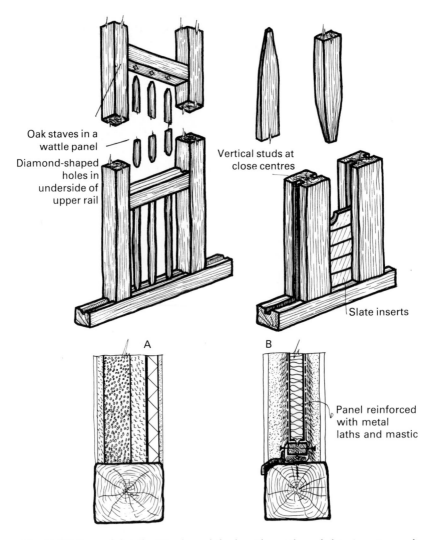

Oak staves in a wattle panel

Diamond-shaped holes in underside of upper rail

Vertical studs at close centres

Slate inserts

A

B

Panel reinforced with metal laths and mastic

Fig 64 **Wall panel details.** Wattle and daub with wattle and slate inserts are shown above. See Fig 44 for wall panel elevation. Alternative recent infill panel methods are shown in (a) and (b). See Figs 66 and 67 for enlarged detail.

roof of a house is equivalent to the contents page of a book; this was never truer than in the case of the timber-framed house in which all of the principal timbers and many of the secondary timbers were essential for the structural rigidity of the frame. In the case of the fully framed house of later date, the first-floor bressummer timbers and the positions of the principal braces are all vitally important to the survey and thus to any subsequent alterations of the building.

In the section dealing with structural elements, a full description was given of essential joints in wall posts, bressummers, plates, sills and braces (see pp22–33). The structural survey will, hopefully, at least highlight the essential joints and indicate to some degree whether or not the connections are secure and intact. Buildings constructed with masonry walls are designed with the walls in compression. This is as a direct result of the forces of gravity and stresses imposed upon the structure. In timber-framed buildings many of the essential structural timbers other than the wall posts are in tension, being the opposite mechanical force. There is a very real danger of failure around the central joints as a result of the structure 'popping' or 'bursting'. This is especially so if an important horizontal timber severs or if a brace fails. In this event the entire structure could begin a toppling motion. Early crown-post construction superseded earlier methods in which bracing was achieved from the outer roof coverings alone.

Once a timber-framed structure has suffered as a result of beam or joint failure, it is extremely difficult and often impossible to restore the position of the failed member. The more usual approach is to strengthen the joints or member with an iron strap or tension plate, and some success has been had using a patent bolt fixing with metal tension plates which are fixed to the top and bottom of a failed beam (see Figs 65, 78–9). The plates act as flanges and the beam as the web or vertical face. The mechanical reaction of the bolts, which pass through the beam and act in compression with the plates, has been found to serve the required purpose of holding, say, a badly damaged collar in one piece. A traditional method of repair is to cut in a further piece of timber to replace the damaged area. This can work very satisfactorily, but when an essential beam is in a state of great tension the physical act of making the new connection can be very difficult.

Metal is frequently used in the repair and maintenance of timber frames, but any person envisaging such a repair should ideally consult a structural engineer first as the section and size of the metal work is structurally crucial to the success of the repair: too small a section of metal brace or strap would perhaps last for a short time but would ultimately burst; too large a section may require extra large holes to be drilled in a timber beam which is not of heavy enough scantling to cope with the alteration. In this case the effect of the proposed cure could well be of greater hazard to the building than the original fault.

A further point to consider is that oak contains a substantial amount of tannic acid and this will in time have an effect upon metal work connected to it, so the metal work must be of sufficient size so as not to be structurally affected by the presence of the tannic acid. The usual metals used in the repair and strengthening of structural timbers in period timber-framed houses are wrought iron and steel. Again, to effect a permanent repair the advice of a structural engineer should be called upon; the cost will be covered by the permanence, performance and success of the repair.

In a timber-framed building the usual defects are as a result of structural distortion in the frame and the resultant cracking and displacement of material forming the infill panels. Distortion in the frame could be very old, caused largely by the use of green wood at the time of the building's construction, which did happen in medieval times. If the frame is warped and twisted but the joints have held and appear to be relatively sound, there may not be too great a problem and action unnecessary in structural terms; but if the joints have opened up and associated timbers are split and obviously defective, there is likely to be evidence of live structural movement in the frame and action will be necessary.

Typical causes of such movement are the cutting of an important part of the timber frame to facilitate the fitting of a door, window or other opening, the removal of essential parts of the frame to provide, for instance, extra space or to allow two rooms to be formed into one. The writer has observed examples where vital braces have been removed to allow chipboard cupboards to be fitted into a bedroom. He has inspected a timber-framed building in Hampshire where the owner decided over a weekend to create an extra studio room in the roof void. Unfortunately, the void was subdivided by two principal collars which spanned the width of the building. The owner wanted one large room and the collars represented what he saw as an inconvenient barrier. He therefore sawed off the collars at the interjunction with the principal rafters and, to add insult to injury, cut up the collars into neat logs to feed his fire! Within one week the building frame had moved as a result of severe roof spread and handmade clay tiles were dropping wholesale on to the paths and surrounding land, some of which formed a public thoroughfare.

The story serves as an example of what structural harm can be done. The removal of wind braces can be fatal to frame construction: the distortions in a frame due to such forces are considerable, and a frame designed to be braced should not, under any circumstances, be

Plate 27a **Decay to sill beams.** This sill beam is badly rotted and should be replaced soon to avoid structural damage of the frame.

Plate 27b **Decay to the sill beam and wall post.** Another example of decay which must be repaired soon.

Plate 28 **Decay to sill beams.** A mid post is affected by decay here. The complete section of sill should be removed to regain stability of the frame.

Plate 29 **A stylobate.** Used to keep the frame above ground level and promote an air space to the underside of the building.

robbed for the sake of convenience. External walls are often covered with claddings which hide wind braces which are passed through slots in the studs and secured to posts, sills and bressummers. It is also common for braces to be halved over intermediate studs and then connected to the other principal timbers with pegged, mortice-and-tenoned joints. These vital connections can be easily damaged by water penetration, causing the joints to rot and break. Shrinkage and decay of timber members will cause tenons to pull away from mortices. Cracks to framed internal partitions can be evidence of hidden braces becoming detached from principal posts and collars. Wherever water attacks timber, rot will occur, and fungal attack, together with wood-boring insects, are major enemies of the timber-framed house. These will be dealt with later.

The timber frame is designed as a stable structure but can only remain so while all of its constituent parts are intact and operable. Rot in sills, posts, braces and bressummers and collars, or the removal of essential parts, will inevitably cause the structure to fail (see Plates 27–9, page 99). It may be that damage to one area of the frame is not obvious and is therefore ignored. A reaction, however, may be set up which manifests itself in part of the structure removed from the root cause of the problem. It is not enough to repair the observed defect; the source of the problem must be found and corrected before further deterioration occurs elsewhere in the structure.

In the writer's own early fifteenth-century house the dining-hall was partly contained within the original timber frame and partly within an extra room in the form of an outshut. The dining-hall was contained at one end of the house and the gable wall was partly of timber-frame construction and partly of brick. At ground level the original frame had been removed on the gable portion and 1ft 1in (32.5cm) of brickwork placed between the original corner posts, which were apparently intact. The gable end was plastered, as were many other houses in the street, most of which were from a later period. It was obvious at the survey that differential movement had taken place at the point at which the brick outshut structure abutted the original rear corner post. As a result, the wall was split from ground to eaves' level on the lower end of the outshut roof, to such an extent that the writer could put his hand through the crack and wriggle it around.

It was also noticed during the survey that a principal collar had split in the roof void; this was structurally related to the corner posts at the front and rear of the gable end. We decided to demolish the badly damaged Victorian outshut gable wall and to rebuild it using fair-faced stock brickwork on the inside, and thermal blockwork on the outside, plastered to match the older part. To our horror we found that the lower portion of the rear corner post was not as it appeared and was, in fact, almost hollow as a result of insect attack and rot. This was caused by water penetration through the external plasterwork and brickwork. Because of complications in the gable wall brickwork and corner post, we were faced with a choice: we could either demolish a large part of the earlier brickwork forming the gable wall so that a new post could be inserted, or we could construct a brick pier under the remains of the corner post to restore the building's structural rigidity. The failure of the post had caused a reaction through the roof which was manifest in the split principal collar. The defect in the post was impossible to see without removal of the gable brickwork, but the survey showed that a problem was likely to be found in another part of the structure because of failure in the roof. We decided to build a pier and made a feature of the detail when the brickwork and the old oak were connected. A damp-proof course should not be forgotten when connecting masonry to timber; we used slate in the example given.

It is therefore vitally important to restore the structural rigidity of a frame to its original form, and this work should take precedence over any cosmetic effects or desire to provide extra living space, door frame openings or fitted cupboards. The medieval builder was proud of his building; its strength and method of construction are the major reasons why so many survive to this day. Up until the middle of the sixteenth century, oak was plentiful and was thus used without concern for quantity by the builders. The principal timbers were usually massive and vastly over-designed, so they are able to take many ignorant alterations and improvements as well as attack from fungi and wood-boring insects. A beam can often be cut near an end without severe danger of structural failure, but the same beam cut in the centre of a span could suffer fatally from the reaction. Consequently, restoration of the frame depends greatly on the design of the structure and the extent to which it has been attacked by man and the elements. Repair of a timber frame is determined to an extent by its function and the degree of damage caused to it. For instance, if the frame is medieval, any replacement timbers should ideally be second-hand from a building of similar age and detail. The timber should, if at all possible, be weathered to the same extent as that which it replaces and most importantly should be of correct scale. Never replace a principal collar of heavy section with one of light section or a heavy post with one of smaller girth. The structural result could be catastrophic and the appearance will be sadly wrong.

If circumstances dictate that new timber is to be used, never mix the types of wood employed. Always put oak with oak and not with a cheaper and perhaps easier-to-come-by alternative. In the house discussed earlier, where the roof collars were cut to facilitate extra roof space, certain first-floor joists were renewed, as was the floor trimmer that bore on the front and rear ground-floor walls. For economy, the original trimmer, which had rotted at the ends, was replaced with green elm, cut only a few weeks earlier on a local landed estate because of Dutch elm disease. A year after installation, the new beam had warped to the shape of a long bow in both the vertical and horizontal plane. The oak first-floor joists were forced to move with the beam, as were the front and rear wall panels, the first-floor stud partitions and the first-floor ceiling joists, rafters and entire roof structure. This movement, together with the spreading roof, meant that the entire building had to be shored up and covered with tarpaulins to stop falling hand-made clay tiles injuring passers-by. The tarpaulins also stopped water penetrating the building through the defective roof coverings. What a disaster a little ignorance and penny-pinching can bring.

The Department of the Environment recommends that new timber should have a moisture content of not more than 15 per cent, which is equal to the usual level of moisture in an existing building. More-over, they say that no timber should be used which has not been kiln-dried, or air-seasoned in its required size, allowing for working tolerances, for at least one year per inch of thickness. It is also impor-tant when jointing a length of new oak to old to take into account the grain of the wood to avoid as much as possible the natural twisting that will inevitably take place after the joint is made.

Medieval oak should not be stained with chemicals to give a desired cosmetic effect. There has been some controversy over the treatments that spliced-in oak should be given. The contemporary vogue is to stain new wood, which is often not even oak or, worse still, is oak look-alike. Mock beams are formed with a scalloped pattern on the face as though this represented an authentic detail. Pubs and restaurants in particular clad their rolled steel joists and steel posts with oak look-alike timber affixed to studding in plank form. The idea is to produce something that looks like a beam or

Plate 30 **A restored fifteenth-century timber-framed house.** Recently restored by a local society and now reused as domestic living accommodation.

post, but is in fact totally unrealistic and very often has the grain running in different and opposing directions. The DoE asks for the adze to be used to achieve a genuine-looking, relatively smooth finish similar to that which a medieval carpenter would have left. The old carpenters' use of the adze gave oak the appearance of being planed, and it is difficult to reproduce this effect today.

With regard to mouldings, there are conflicting views on treatments which can be divided simply into two groups. The Society for the Protection of Ancient Buildings recommend that whenever old timbers contain mouldings, new timbers should be worked simply, without enrichment which might compete with the old work (see Plate 30). It also says that when new timber replaces decayed wood, it should not be carved like the old and that only main mouldings should be repeated. This view is in line with the society's manifesto which broadly states that restoration should be confined to essential repairs carried out in a manner whereby no attempt should be made to produce vanished details. The DoE, however, says that mouldings should be cut oversized and then finished on the carpenter's bench to avoid any appearance of machine working. The fact that this gives a licence to age timber artificially does not seem to cause any concern.

Oak, like any other timber, is in danger of weathering on its exposed faces. The main danger points are horizontal areas such as ledges or sills and bressummers. The underside of a sill and the vertical joint between a panel and a stud are also main danger areas. If a new horizontal timber is added and the grain is close, the upper surface may be lightly planed to form a weathering in order to shed surface water. If the grain is not sufficiently close, then water may penetrate the wood and rot it. The best alternative where a horizontal member projects beyond the face of a panel is to cover it in 4lb lead flashing. In more exposed conditions, 5lb lead may be best. This can be taken up under a panel of wattle and daub or tucked into the nearest brick joint if the panel is brick (see Fig 73).

A well-maintained oak frame should resist decay by natural weathering and it is surprising how much wood can deteriorate without adverse effect on the strength of the structure. When originally constructed, strong reliance was placed on brickwork or masonry below the sill beam to provide a damp course. We now know that brickwork alone is inadequate to provide a satisfactory damp course and so it is strongly recommended that a new sill beam be bedded on lead, 5lb lead being best in this respect.

It is often possible to slide lead under an old existing sill beam to offer it protection from rising dampness; often, the old oak will be in remarkably good condition and it is worth the effort to extend its life. If intermediate panels are finished flush with the outside face of framing, a water check can be formed within the thickness of the panel by bedding in mastic and screwed oak fillets to form a water drip. The inevitable shrinkage problem between panels and framing can be alleviated using mastic pointing, and alternatives are described later in this chapter with regard to alternative panel materials (see Figs 66 and 67).

When inspecting a wall frame for repair, it is always a good idea to start at the rear of the building and work round to the sides, saving the front until last. The reason for this is that all the nasty bits are normally hidden away as much as possible, and the rear, or least looked at side, is best for this purpose! For instance, plumbing pipework is not normally made a feature of. Drain runs, soil and vent pipes, rain-water down-pipes, exposed cables, etc are best put on the rear elevation where perhaps the elevation is plainer. Climbing roses, wisteria, honeysuckle and clematis are more likely to be found at the front of the house where impact is most important.

As a result, neglect of the essential fabric is more likely to be found at the rear than on more exposed sides open to view. With period timber-framed houses, aspect is also important. Which way does the house face and which way do the prevailing winds and rain project? Look at the exposed and weathered faces first if you like, but leave the best, least exposed or most attractive face till last. The frame, if exposed, is open to wind, driving rain, frost and hot sunshine. Properly protected and regularly maintained and repaired, the period timber-framed house will last as long as any solid brick or stone building. It is, of course, essential to ensure that roof coverings are in good order and that rain-water disposal methods are adequate. These, if defective, will result in a structurally unsound frame in a surprisingly short time.

No matter in which direction the house faces, north is likely to be a relatively sheltered side. This elevation rarely gets the benefit of sunshine and driving rain is likely to be minimal. If the frame is exposed on the north side, then it is likely to be in reasonable condition and relatively unweathered. When inspecting a house for the first time, look at the north side first because here the structure is likely to be untampered with. Old plaster coating, limewashing or other external weather treatment is likely to be on view here. The sun, wind and rain will not have had the opportunity of greatly changing the appearance of the external finishes. Any original external limewash over the structural frame may be visible, as will any attempt to weatherproof the wall.

The east face is open to a little exposure with a relatively weak morning sun and drizzly rain. Heavy rain from the east is infrequent and any wind is mild. Often when it rains from the east, moist air is accompanied by a wind which can in time penetrate the essential structure of a timber frame.

The face of a period timber-framed house likely to suffer the most is the south. On summer days the frame is exposed to the full blast of a hot summer sun. This causes the timber to shrink and mortice-and-tenon joints to open up. Rain from the south and south-west is often driving in force and wind blows the water into previously shrunken joints where it percolates through the wood and into joints and wall-panel connections. Cracks and shakes in the frame, opened up during hot summer months, now provide ideal ground for rot to develop. The problem is compounded by surface water driven onto the walls and running down part and full height posts to the joints between these and ground sills or bressummers. Water is drawn into the frame by capillary action and tenons are rotted as a result. Frame posts rot from the bottom upwards and cause subsequent instability in the structure as a whole (see Plates 27–9). The west face suffers in the same way but to a lesser extent. Driving rain is far more frequent from the west than the east, and on a sunny day temperature is likely to be greater on the west face than the east.

Wall-frame restoration or repair is usually concerned with the cutting out of defective vertical or horizontal members, either in mid-span or at a joint. The writer has carried out a number of surveys on timber-framed houses where wall frames have been repaired or at least repairs have been attempted. For instance, at a joint between a wall post and bressummer beam, it is common to see failure of the tenon, or 'springing' of the joint, as a result of movement in the building and failure of the trenails or pegs. At a fifteenth-century hall house, this defect had been repaired by fastening a plate of steel about 6in sq (152mm sq) and ¼in (6mm) thick across the joint (see Fig 65). The steel plate was drilled with four holes to take coach bolts which passed through the plate and into the oak frame. Two bolts attached the plate to the vertical post and the others to the bressummer. The 'plated' joint was apparently about thirty years old and appeared to be standing up to its situation well. The metal was treated with red lead paint on both sides and regularly black painted with bitumastic paint as a protection against rust. Visible sections of the bolts appeared sound, but tannic acid could well have attacked metal buried in the woodwork. If such a repair is envisaged, then it would be worthwhile treating the bolts with red lead or some other preservative in order to extend their useful life. Bolts made of an acid-resistant alloy, or galvanised steel, would be best.

Plate repairs such as that just discussed are also common at the connections between vertical studs and mid-rails, or studs and sill beams. The repair is also effective where a vertical post or strut connects to a wall plate at eaves' level. Longitudinal movement in a wall frame often has the effect of bursting a frame at the mortice-and-tenon joint. Another effective repair using metal is the blacksmith's strap and many of these can be found on period timber-framed houses which were identified as defective during Victorian times. The strap consists of an iron strip, perhaps 2in (50mm) wide × ¼in (6mm) thick and 1½–2ft (450–600mm) in length. Many such straps seen by the writer have square-shaped holes punched in them,

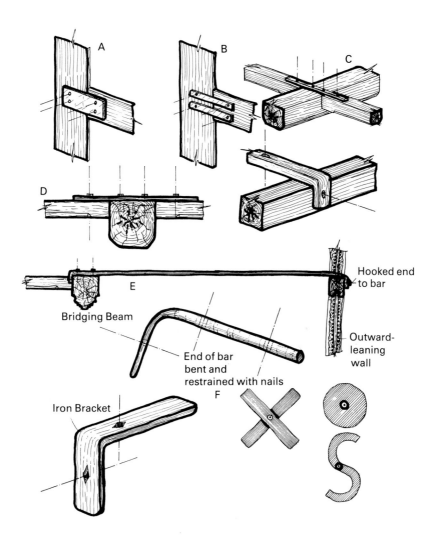

Fig 65 **Metal straps and bars.** A variety of straps and bars used to rectify exploded joints and leaning walls. A) Metal plate repair at a vertical post/rail junction. B) A similar repair to A using straps. C) A common strap repair to a bridging beam/joist connection. D) Typical section of strap repair to bridging beam/joist. E) A blacksmith's bar to restrain an outward leaning wall. F) Various common wall plate patterns of restraining bars for outward leaning walls.

through which stout iron nails or bolts pass into the oak frame. At a defective joint between an interrupted mid-rail and a post (see Fig 65), the strap is fixed to the outside of the frame. It is attached to the mid-rail, the post and the next portion of mid-rail holding the three elements together to form a cross. The defective section of panel is then restrained by both the post and the next sound section of panel of which the adjoining mid-rail is part.

The same repair can be used where a post connecting to a sill beam has rotted at the base and lateral movement is possible. It is, however, vitally important to ensure that sufficient sound wood is present at the base of the post so that it can sit on the sill without downward movement (see Fig 65).

Outward-leaning walls are a common defect in period timber-framed houses. In brick or stone buildings, outward-leaning movement is a problem often solved with metal tie-bars passing right through the structure to the wall opposite. The theory is that the opposite wall will restrain such movement and usually end walls, such as gables, act as ribs, further aiding support. It is also common for tie-bar rods to be used in period timber-framed houses and here, the rod may pass through the building or be restrained on an internal bridging beam or bressummer running parallel with the defective wall. Where this occurs it is common to find the end of the bar nearest the beam flattened out and hammered into the shape of a hook or bent through 90°. The end is then hooked over the bridging beam and usually nailed into place via a hole cut in the flattened end of the rod for this purpose (see Fig 65). The use of metal tie-rods, plates, bars and brackets is common, but it must be acknowledged that the introduction of metal into the external parts of a period timber frame can cause more problems. For example, a long metal rod can expand and contract according to changes in temperature and this is especially important when the rod is in excess of about 30ft (9.1m) in length. Short rods can be used to brace outward-leaning walls and the writer has recently seen an adjustable rod, threaded and with a large wing nut provided to counteract movement in the frame.

On a more traditional level, wall-frame repairs can be made by reproducing the art of the medieval carpenter. Plates 31 and 32 show wall-frame repairs carried out at a private house and the Weald and Downland Open Air Museum at Singleton in Sussex. Wall-frame timbers most likely to be in need of repair are posts especially at low level where they connect to a sill beam. The sill beam itself may have rotted in mid-section either near or remote from a scarf joint; a post and mid-rail connection as a result of water penetration and rot; and the wall plate may have rotted in a local area owing to faulty rain-water goods or where an existing scarf joint has moved sideways as a result of roof spread.

Dealing with these in order, traditional repairs may be carried out as follows.

WALL-POST AND SILL-BEAM JOINTS

This is probably the most likely failure as a result of driving rain, percolating water and on a south-facing wall shrinkage of the joint owing to sunshine and heat. Owing to the fact that the sill beam is lying flat with the grain horizontal, it is possible that the sill timber is sound enough in condition to be left (see Plates 27–32). Any decayed outer wood should be trimmed off and the member treated with a proprietary brand of clear preservative chemical. If it is possible to do so, then a lead damp-proof course should be slipped under the sill to help prevent rising water further attacking the wood. It will be necessary to test the wall post with a sharp implement in order to assess the extent of rot and savable timber. A post should never be cut out entirely merely to create an easier repair. In many cases it will be tempting to do this and often it will be the only sensible course of action. The writer was forced by circumstances to remove the entire bottom section of a post up to bressummer level. The post was rotted to a height of about 5ft (1.5m) above ground level and in poor condition for the remaining portion up to just below bressummer level. The mortice-and-tenon joint at bressummer level was in sound condition and subsequently saved. In this case the repair was in the form of a brick pier capped with a damp course and upon which the post stub sat. For the purpose of these notes, however, we will assume that a new section of oak is used to replace that which is rotted and that the frame is open to view. The writer would suggest that the post be cut at the point where sound timber is found. If the post is a principal, then obviously some form of propping will be necessary while the defective or rotted timber is cut out, otherwise an element of instability will occur in the frame as a whole. If an internal bridging beam or bressummer connects to the post at a higher level than the repair, then it may be possible to restrain the post by propping the other beam with 'Acrow' or similar adjustable props. It may be necessary to 'pin up' the structure using two sets of props, one internally, one externally for the duration of the repair. Once the structure is adequately propped, the sawn off post should be cut further to form an elongated tongue (see Plates 31–2). A section of new oak, or similar scantling, should be selected and cut to match the existing post. The new member should be cut to form a socket into

Plate 31 **Wall post restoration.** A well restored corner post and sill beam. Note the attention to detail at timber scantling and grain match.
Plate 32 **Wall post restoration.** Another restored wall post on a wattle and daub clad building.

which the tongue of the existing post might fit. The reader will note that a splay is formed in the short cuts of the existing post and that these are matched in the new member. This joinery detail will effectively lock the existing post into the new member and will facilitate the new member being edged into position when bearing in mind that a further tongue or tenon must be negotiated at the joint with the sill beam. Once fully located, the entire joint can be pinned together with trenails.

An alternative wall-post repair uses a simple stepped joint suitable for lengthening members wholly in compression. Once again, this repair is commonly carried out in conjunction with the renewal of a section of ground sill. Plate 31 shows a new section of post together with a repaired portion of ground sill. The sill joint is in the form of a longitudinal bevelled dovetail halving, being traditional in this connection, and which also may be used for joining sections of a wall plate. A wall plate, however, like a ground sill, is a rigid member and should not, under any circumstances, be cut or weakened by insufficient jointing of new sections when these are inserted.

In order to make the wall-post step-joint repair, the extent of

110

sound wood should be determined and the structure 'pinned' to avoid movement. The lower rotted section can be cut out and a step joint formed in the base of the remaining existing post as illustrated. A matching section of timber of similar scantling should be cut to form the new member and, if necessary, a new section of sill beam. Post and sill beam mortice-and-tenon joints should be cut and the sill offered into place. The step-joint repair in the post should be located and pegged back into place with a trenail.

SILL BEAMS

A rotted sill beam will manifest other defects in the wall frame. If a principal post is located near the point of rot, then downward movement of the post might occur because in effect, the sill beam is a foundation for the wall-frame members. The defect may occur below a large square wattle-and-daub panel and away from any principal upright posts. The wattle panel is woven around staves, usually of oak, which are wedged vertically between the sill and the next mid-rail (see Fig 64, p96). Rot at the sill will cause the staves to work loose and eventually to drop, with subsequent failure of the panel.

The medieval carpenter used scarf joints to connect two sections of sill beam and any repair should match existing joints in other parts of the frame. If we assume that rot has occurred in the sill at the base of a post, but the post is not yet affected, the following repair may be suitable. The post will need 'pinning' in order to avoid loading at the joint with the sill beam. Once frame loadings are relieved, any wall panel adjacent to the sill will have to be removed either in part or wholly in order to facilitate cutting of the defective sill timber. If the sill is elevated on a dwarf wall of brick or stone, then it may be possible to remove part of this beneath the sill so that the defective member can drop out into the space provided. In any circumstances, the manoeuvre of actually removing the sill is likely to be difficult and great care and patience is necessary so that damage to other parts of the frame is avoided.

A new section of timber should be prepared and great care taken as to its exact cross-sectional size as this will be important in relocating the member beneath the wall post. Any mortice sockets should be formed as necessary and a stave groove or hole cut to match the existing sill ready to accommodate the existing post and staves. On completion of this work, the sill should be offered up into the required space and the tenon of the post located accordingly. Scarf joints cut

111

Plate 33 **Roof repairs.** A repair to a wall plate using a scarfing joint.
Plate 34 **Roof repairs.** A beautiful repair to a wall plate using new oak. Note the metal holding pins later to be replaced with trenails.

to match those of the existing building should line up and be connected (see Plate 33). This complete, the under-walling should be rebuilt, the trenails hammered home, pinning removed and any making good carried out as necessary.

Should the area of rot be located in a mid-panel, then the above procedure can be followed, but pinning of the vertical members may not be necessary. Once again, it is strongly advised to insert a lead damp-proof course beneath the repaired section and if possible to all parts of the frame below sill level. All leadwork should be treated properly with paint to protect it against the decaying effects of tannic acid.

WALL PLATES OR TOP PLATES

Like sill beams, wall plates are rigid members and should not be weakened with any unnecessary cutting or jointing. Many roof trusses rest on the wall plate and loadings are considerable. In order that continuity of structure is gained at eaves' level, complicated halved, bevelled and dove-tailed lengthening joints are used and it is essential that repairs are to a similar standard. The wall-plate repair joint shown in Plate 34 is perhaps the most suitable to ensure that the building does not buckle outward in a horizontal plane and is able to withstand thrust from any inadequately tied rafters. The wall plate in a period timber-framed building is always a substantial timber

112

and its function demands that it is maintained in sound condition.

Rot in a wall plate is commonly caused by leaking rain-water goods, which in time penetrate any timber members adjacent to the eaves. It is therefore imperative that gutters and down-pipes be repaired and maintained to avoid water leakage and ingress to the essential framing of the building.

JOINTS

Failure of individual framing members will cause instability of the structure, but failure at the joints is equally, if not more, serious. The joints most prone to damage are those at the eaves and apex of a roof where dampness, fungal and insect attack are greatest. Wall joints may be faulty as a result of pressure or movement in the frame either natural or unnatural. As we have discussed, renewal of a frame member often necessitates the renewal of a joint. The wall-post sill-beam repair is a case in point. In addition to forming new wall-post and sill-beam joints, the connecting mortice and tenon had to be replaced.

Function is perhaps a key word here. The repair must enable the member and joint to perform the function for which it was originally intended by the medieval carpenter. Any repair necessitates the removal of the damaged area of timber and its replacement by other timber of similar scantling and character to the original. The grain must lie in the same direction as the original and the face of the new timber must be on the same plane as that of the old to gain continuity in the structure. Any joint must be actually fitted together to transfer any loadings along the member.

A repair usually involves removal of the damaged timber, although sometimes the defect may be made good and the member replaced. If decay of a member affects the whole of a joint, then it will need replacement, but often only part of a joint is affected, in which case repair may be possible. As an example, a decayed tenon may be sawn off an otherwise sound beam. A mortice may be formed in the old wood and a false tenon inserted, pinned at both ends. Alternatively, the old member may form part of a renewed section of timber. Often it will be necessary to form a deep mortice in the old timber to allow the false tenon to slide into position and be wedged tight when fully located. Such repairs can be seen at the Weald and Downland Open Air Museum at Singleton in West Sussex. If the insertion is only the tenon, one end only should be glued in the false mortice in order that any gaps can be made up. The actual joint itself should be pinned only with trenails to allow for natural structural movement in the frame as a whole.

A similar repair can be made to the defective or rotted walls of a mortice socket. New timber can be inserted against the old and glued into place to complete the joint. A repair of this nature is especially suitable for collar and rafter joints, purlin to principal rafter joints, and in wall panels the connection between a wall plate and a tie-beam. It is, however, important to look carefully at the extent of rot or decay in original timber as this will determine the amount of original wood to be cut away. While repairs of this nature are pre-ferred, they are not always possible and metal straps or flitch plates are the best alternative (see Figs 65 pp107, 78–9 pp 158–60).

It is also important to note that any pegging of a joint should be carried out with care in order to avoid splitting of a member along the grain. Pegs should be staggered in order to avoid this risk. In forming any joint in oak, it is important that any cuts are made as near as possible at a right angle to the grain to avoid splitting. The Department of the Environment recommends that when members are repaired or joined, pins or trenails should not be relied upon in total for strength at the joint. They recommend the use of waterproof glue together with pins.

Medieval buildings were nearly always built of green oak which can warp and twist to a considerable extent. Much of the distortion seen in medieval houses today is as a result of this old movement. The medieval carpenters used flexible joints to counteract this movement and a person should not be unduly alarmed at the slope of a wall panel which may appear, to say the least, dramatic. It is, however, possible that distortion of the panel is as a result of frame failure and close examination of the joints and members will indicate whether or not this is the case.

WALL-FRAME DISTORTION

Part of the charm of a period timber-framed house is the undulating line of oak beams, seemingly toppling towards or away from the chimney stack – the bressummer beam which at one end of the house is 8ft (2.4m) above ground level, and at the other end 7½ft (2.2m), and the windows which lean to the side and outwards. These are all features which we look for and which cannot be reproduced in modern houses.

114

It is, however, wise to inspect thoroughly the wall-frame structure to ensure that the toppling is in character only and not a likely occurrence of decay. Principal causes of such distortion are failure of members owing to decay, the effects of rot and wood-boring insects on joints, and the cutting of framed members to insert chimney stacks, windows, staircases and doors. Many wholly timber-framed buildings include hidden braces which may be halved over the back of studs and concealed internally with plaster linings, plasterboard sheeting and decorative finishes. Externally, the braces may be hidden by internal panel infilling. If such a defect is found to exist, the exact cause should be established and steps taken to carry out any necessary repairs.

Such a failure may be difficult to diagnose, dependent upon its nature, but a sure sign that such a defect is present would be the progressive movement of the building which may manifest itself internally with cracks in cosmetic finishes. If such movement is present in a period timber-framed house, monitoring of the movement is essential to establish a rate of movement. The use of glass tell-tales adhesed to the wall panels may help establish a rate of movement. If it can be established that progressive movement does not exist, then it may be advisable to make good any damage that may have occurred but leave the frame intact. The writer has, however, experienced circumstances where a timber-framed building had moved to an alarming extent and, while no obvious damage had occurred to individual members or joints, the building was on an inconvenient slope in which to live! It was, for example, impossible to find a relatively level floor surface at first-floor level and the amount of slope was inconveniently extreme. In this case the building was jacked up very carefully to a more reasonable level and the joints became better formed as a result. Internal floor levels were still extremely undulating, but at least the building was habitable.

Period timber-framed houses are constructed in such a way that they could be taken apart rather like Meccano, and re-erected on another site if so desired. Country magazines often carry advertisements for dismantled barns or Wealden houses, ready for re-erection and conversion to a house, on a site chosen by the purchaser. Dismantling of the frame also means that members can be taken out and replaced, which is obviously an advantage in this type of construction, although drastic.

Early roofs were designed to exert a side thrust to the upper parts of side walls. The tie-beam was omitted to create an open roof, but walls tended to suffer as a result. Movement in the tops of side walls will also ultimately distort roof trusses which are in effect being spread at the joint with the side-wall panel. The answer is perhaps to strengthen the side-wall panels, in which case the writer would recommend that specialist advice be sought as the problem is complex and beyond the immediate scope of this book.

Framed members and joints hidden from view behind distorted wall panels can be repaired in much the same way as has been described for joints and members on view. Some hidden repairs may make use of metal bars, straps or plates and softwood may even be considered (see Fig 65). Steel plates with bolt heads and nuts can be left on view without distracting from the appearance of the building and, in addition, strapping to reinforce joints is acceptable. Any repaired distorted wall-frame panels should be properly prepared and any large gaps or voids filled to stop water creeping in and causing rot, insect attack and further damage.

REPAIRS TO WALL-FRAME JOINTS AND MEMBERS USING PLASTIC

So far we have discussed repairs to framing members and joints using traditional methods of scarfing new timber to replace rotted or otherwise defective wood. We have looked at the use of metal as a reinforcement both traditionally and as a repair. We now live in a society where plastics play an important role. Systems have been developed both in this country and overseas for the restoration of structural timber members and joints using plastic as an alternative material. Some examples of repair using plastic are discussed and Figs 66–7 demonstrate the text.

Rotted beam end This defect may occur at the end of a joist, bressummer sill or wall plate (see Fig 68). The first stage is to remove any badly rotted wood which, despite appearance, is unlikely to have any mechanical strength. Timber adjacent to the beam end and only partly rotted is unlikely to provide adequate strength and will have doubtful mechanical properties. Soft timber should be removed, leaving only the core of sound wood which will eventually become more mechanically important further in from the beam end. Holes of 28mm diameter should be drilled into the top of the member at an angle of about 20° from the sides and polyester reinforcement bars of about 20mm diameter are inserted into the holes. Epoxy mortar is

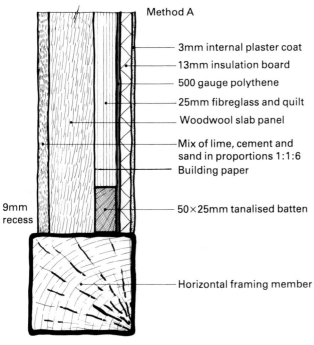

Method A

- 3mm internal plaster coat
- 13mm insulation board
- 500 gauge polythene
- 25mm fibreglass and quilt
- Woodwool slab panel
- Mix of lime, cement and sand in proportions 1:1:6
- Building paper

9mm recess

- 50×25mm tanalised batten

- Horizontal framing member

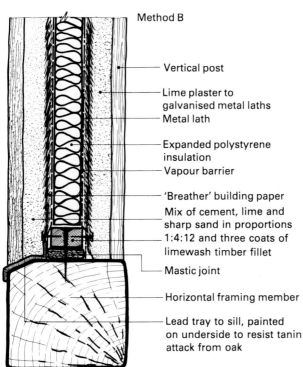

Method B

- Vertical post
- Lime plaster to galvanised metal laths
- Metal lath
- Expanded polystyrene insulation
- Vapour barrier
- 'Breather' building paper
- Mix of cement, lime and sharp sand in proportions 1:4:12 and three coats of limewash timber fillet
- Mastic joint

- Horizontal framing member

- Lead tray to sill, painted on underside to resist tanin attack from oak

Fig 66 **Alternative infill panel. Method A.** Recommended by the SPAB good thermal insulation can be achieved by this and the alternative shown in Fig 67.
Fig 67 **Alternative infill panel. Method B.** See Fig 66.

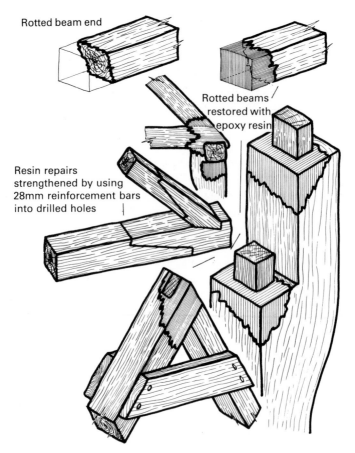

Rotted beam end

Rotted beams
restored with
epoxy resin

Resin repairs
strengthened by using
28mm reinforcement bars
into drilled holes

Fig 68 **Repairs using epoxy resin.** Typical instances where epoxy resin can be used. If necessary the resin can be reinforced by drilling into the member and inserting 28mm reinforcement bars.

used to fill any cavities and to form a 'plastic foot' in the space where the wood was rotted. Epoxy resin is used to form an unbreakable adhesive between the reinforcement rods and any sound wood remaining. It is also important to note that epoxy resin is moisture resistant and therefore the rotting process is halted on application of this repair. Drill holes remain hidden from view as they are applied to the top of the beam and the appearance of the member remains unchanged.

Joints Using the principles just discussed, it is possible to re-form a timber joint in plastic using the plastic as an alternative to any rotted timber in the member. Fig 68 illustrates possible uses of plastic in joint repair. We have discussed the importance of framing members as constituent parts of a structure and the necessity of joints being able to move freely at connecting points. Repairs using plastic do allow for a certain amount of freedom in movement, but often a frame will have to be dismantled in part in order that the defective member can be made accessible. Plastic repairs are a suitable way of building decayed sections of timber and the finished moulding can closely resemble the shape of timber it replaces. Such a repair can also be used in restoration of floor structures where the use of steel may be inconvenient or even impossible.

All this is based on the premise that the timber frame in question is worth saving, and that the amount of decay has not reached such an extent that it would be more prudent to renew the member completely. Period timber-framed houses which have survived to this day are generally, especially the older ones, of a good standard and built using scantlings of substance. Local authority planning departments are especially keen to ensure that historic buildings of all categories are preserved, but extra care may be taken in the case of timber-framed buildings. However, owing to financial restraints, the average timber-framed house, while perhaps listed, is not always given the attention it deserves from the local authority who may have more exceptional buildings in their care that demand attention. This has been reflected in the attitude of local authorities to grant applications.

One viewpoint, arguably wrong, is that the period timber-frame building does not come up to contemporary standards because, for instance, it may not have the minimum facilities, WCs, bathrooms, kitchen equipment or similar present-day requirements. Not so long ago, the timbered house was the subject of ardent attack because it failed, for instance, under the by-laws and Building Regulations regarding head-room and similar contemporary standards. Such seemingly ridiculous arguments actually condemned large numbers of timbered buildings to demolition.

In addition to the public health, by-law and Building Regulations arguments, those interested in restoration have had a fight on their hands with other sections. There were, and indeed still are, those who believe that timber-framed buildings harbour disease and that the framework can only be temporary as in time it is bound to decay and rot. In fact, the period timber-framed house is a very flexible object when built in its original form of adaptable and natural materials. The oak structural frame is in every sense of the word a massively strong object which, when well maintained, will outlast many other modern building materials.

It has been said that an oak frame can last longer structurally in a fire than, for instance, a contemporary steel frame, the reason being that a steel frame heats up to a point at which the metal becomes soft and pliable and may even melt. At the moment of pliability the frame will fail. The timber frame, when of oak, will obviously burn, but because of the nature of the material the combustion is very slow and smouldering, and it has been proved that the steel frame will fail first. Oak is an organic material and can therefore decay with age and neglect. Critics of the material use this as an objection, but the claim is manifestly untrue when a structure of sound timber has been well maintained. The woodwork in many surviving medieval houses is in exceptionally sound condition.

It was said earlier that unfeeling alteration is a major cause of failure in the structural frame, and this is evidenced in examples throughout the country. As an example, the writer once visited a timber-framed house in Hampshire which had been altered dramatically and unsympathetically at the beginning of this century. The alterations included the removal of a principal structural wall post which just happened to be where the owner wanted a door opening. The new door could easily have been placed elsewhere, but at the expense of the structural frame the post was lopped off to bressummer level. Other extensions to the property, including an outshut, effectively propped the dismembered frame, but owing to gravity, the structure sank on the altered side and caused other structural problems of a reaction type in other parts of the building.

In another example a survey was being carried out on a timber-framed building which had 9in (22.5cm) brick walls of Victorian origin added at ground-floor level. The detail allowed for the wall posts and ground sills to be hidden away behind brickwork and internal timber panelling. Unfortunately, there was no damp-proof course and in addition a stone sink unit nearby had leaked for several years. Dry-rot had taken a hold on the hidden oak frame as a result, and also from rising dampness in the Victorian wall. The internal wall panelling made a moist, dark and warm breeding ground for fungus to thrive. The entire frame at ground level and immediately above had to be taken out, causing the owner much distress and financial burden. In the remaining ground-floor areas of the house, the posts and sills were largely exposed and above floor level the problems described could not have been less likely or expected.

Exposure of the frame was the original intent and with regular maintenance the structure should have remained in good order.

There used to be an argument in favour of destroying the timber frame as a result of a change in aesthetic fashion. This happened when, in the nineteenth century, the country farmhouse-type of property came to be regarded as picturesque. The idea set up the counter argument condemning the timber frame as lacking in solid and worthy qualities. This argument may exist today in very limited quarters, but the writer has never heard it openly expressed. It was suggested that the medieval timber-framed house was an object for observation by the archaeologist. This, it was said, he should do while the building was in the process of demolition. Hopefully that viewpoint is also dead. Some would have it that any buildings worthy of restoration have now been restored, and what we pass on as a heritage to our sons and daughters is largely fake. It is true that our forefathers overdid the fake work and that sometimes genuine old work was removed only to be replaced by a conjectural restoration in the style of the earlier parts of the building.

Thankfully, in the late nineteenth century, William Morris and others led a reaction against this policy and in 1877 founded the Society for the Protection of Ancient Buildings. The society believed that restoration should be confined to essential repairs carried out in an honest manner with no attempts to reproduce vanished features. Although damage has occurred to timber buildings, its quantity should not be exaggerated and a vast amount of original work still survives today. A criticism which the writer believes has merit is that the fashion to stain old oak with creosote, Cuprinol or other types of wood preservative/stain is unwarranted. When a timber-frame building is restored, it is likely that a considerable number of timbers will be exposed, some of which will be in better condition than others. It is tempting under these circumstances to stain all visible woodwork with a dark stain to form a cosmetic contrast with white emulsioned walls. There may also be a desire to tone down and perhaps standardise the colour of the wood, which will probably vary considerably in colour, dependent upon the atmosphere and the degree of its protection and subjection to light.

Wherever possible, the wood should be maintained in its original form and any protective fluids applied should be of a clear type. The grain of oak in particular is at its very best when, after long exposure, it has turned to a silvery hue. It seems a travesty to ruin this natural attractive tone with a twentieth-century chemical. In addition to stain, some of which may be protective, oil may be rubbed into the wood, both internally and externally. The effect the oil has on natural wood is harmful because, in addition to causing it to change colour unnaturally, the oil also collects harmful dirt. Old oak is valuable and should be properly maintained. The correct way to do this is to clean thoroughly the surface of the wood and rub in beeswax and white spirit. This treatment is intended for internal oak which, as a result of modern central heating systems, has dried out. External wood is best treated against attack by a proprietary brand of preservative, but of a clear type.

Shakes or cracks in external timbers can lodge surface water and thus accelerate rot. The natural elasticity of the timber makes it less likely to be adversely affected by frost, and the wood is not sufficiently porous for water to soak in to any great extent. When dealing with decay in old external oak, it is as well to remember that the scantlings used are generally of large section and so have a substantial safety factor built into them, perhaps unwittingly, by our forefathers. It is possible to cut away a considerable quantity of decayed wood and still be left with a member of more than adequate strength to do the job for which it was provided. If the damage is local and it is at all possible, the repair should be effected by a patch of similar wood in a matching style.

All English oak has shakes which to the layman may appear quite alarming, but beams of an early medieval house are centuries old and, if looked after, can survive for many more centuries. A detail often seen in restoration but despised by many restorers is the practice of filling shakes with cement or caulking. If the owner feels it absolutely necessary to fill them, hemp set in mastic can be used, but as a rule always allow the wood to have its natural way and do not try to disguise its peculiarities. It never works.

Another detail often seen is the filling of old mortices. Many timbers used, even in early medieval building, were second-hand and had already had a life of indeterminate length and usage. The timbers may well be older than the building itself and dendrochronological tests on some old timbers give surprising results. Commonly, old floor beams are reused as posts, and the mortice slots still appear although turned through 90°. Similarly, original principal posts and collars may show the tell-tale signs of being second-hand. The odd slot or unused mortice, set at an angle which could never have had a purpose in this building, is very common and adds interest to the structure, also indicating a re-use of materials.

Cement renderings Very often the old plaster coverings of a timber-framed building will have been replaced by stiff, brittle cement renderings. The old plaster could flex and take up movement in the natural frame, but inelastic rendering is unable to do this and cracks as a result. Gaps occur around the edges of the panels through which water can penetrate and cause damage. Cracks of this nature should be filled with lime, sand and cement mortar. The addition of lime will give the filler a natural elasticity. The external timbers should be regularly treated with a clear external quality fungicide/insecticide but should never be dark stained, varnished, painted or treated with any impervious coatings. Most reputable timber infestation companies will advise on treatment and the reader would be well advised to consult and perhaps purchase the appropriate chemical from such a company.

Plaster pargeting Many timber-framed buildings are clad in plaster pargeting which can be limewashed regularly to maintain its appearance. When the pargeting becomes damaged, it should be repaired using lime and sand plaster mixed in the proportion of one part lime to three parts sand. If it is necessary to repair the laths, new strips of similar size and section should be obtained and set at approximately ⅜in (9mm) centres. When a surveyor carries out an inspection of a building which incorporates this detail, he would do well to inspect the most neglected elevations from which he might learn the most about the construction of the building. These are likely to be the most weathered and the construction may be partially exposed or bared here.

It is often the case today that an enthusiastic restorer, believing he is acting by the very best principles, will hack off plaster pargeting from the external wall panels in the belief that he is exposing the original structure below. In reality, plaster was much used during the seventeenth and eighteenth centuries and as such might well have been applied over the original panels of much older buildings. In many more cases, however, the timber frame, which it is now fashionable to expose at all costs, was not intended for display so the plaster coating was the finish intended by the original builder. The reasons for applying plaster were twofold: first, in terms of comfort value, a thin walled building with gaps between the panels and the structural timber frame was draughty, cold and let in the damp.

Secondly, the timber frame was, to an extent, regarded as a poor man's structure and had derogative connotations in a changing and more affluent society. If it were possible to disguise the exposed frame and infill panels, it was certainly considered by some to be socially desirable to do so. Plasterwork was often decorated and of a good quality, but the contemporary fashion to expose the structural frame entails the destruction of this plasterwork. To restore a pargeted wall panel, the original plaster should be preserved at all costs, unless it is causing structural damage to the timber frame or is impeding necessary structural works by its presence.

One of the main problems with plaster is that it becomes detached from timber work underneath and is then said to be 'live'. We have said that riven laths should be used because they flex with the structural frame, but it should be noted that the nails which fix the laths to the frame are likely to be affected by tannic acid in the wood. It is therefore important to ensure that any nails used are able to resist tannic acid. Galvanised or alloy nails are perhaps the best in this respect. Plaster becomes detached when, as the result of neglected and unfilled cracks, water penetrates the space between it and the timber work. Two things can then happen: first, the laths are liable to rot and this, together with the effect of tannic acid on the nails, causes the plaster to become detached; secondly, water penetrating the plaster will form a thin skin behind the coating and in winter is liable to freeze. The consequent expansion and contraction is enough to blow the plaster away from the structure to which it should be attached. It is sometimes possible, when attempting to restore a plaster panel, to screw it back into place, ensuring that the face is not further damaged by doing so. To do this, brass screws set with zinc or copper washers can be used with good results. The washers prevent the screw head penetrating and damaging the plaster while pressure is applied. If the screw head and washers are counter-sunk fixed, the completed fixing can be quite easily plastered over and thus hidden from view.

Wattle-and-daub panels The oldest method of panel infilling is perhaps the one most associated with period timber-framed build-ings: wattle and daub. This took different forms dependent upon the design of the structural frame. In earlier houses, when timber was more plentifully used, the vertical walling studs were set at close centres and usually rose to the full height of a storey. The resultant panel was tall and narrow in form. Split oak laths were cut to a length at which they were just too long to fit across the panel, and grooves were cut on the inside faces of the vertical members (see Fig 64 p96). Oak laths were then sprung into the grooves, often in a not very regular pattern. When timber became scarcer in the eighteenth century it became necessary to widen the centres between the vertical studs and to introduce horizontal members into the framing to produce squarer shaped panels. Horizontal timbers, such as sills and bressummers, were drilled with holes to take the ends of vertically mounted staves of split oak. These were cut slightly longer than the space between the panels to allow the staves to be sprung into the holes. Hazel strips were then woven between the oak staves to form the wattle. An alternative to hazel strips was the use of laths tied to the staves with leather thongs.

The daub comprised a mixture of cow hair, straw and flax mixed with wet clay until it was suitably sticky and pliable (see Appendix 2). The builder would then literally throw the daub into the wattle frame from both sides until the panel was of a suitable thickness. The mixture dried fairly quickly, and when thoroughly dry was given a coat of lime/hair plaster to fill up any cracks and crevices. This treatment also had the effect of waterproofing the panel and helping to stop excessive shrinkage, which would have occurred if the daub itself had been the surface exposed to weathering. The wattle-and-daub panel is very effective for the purpose intended, and many period timber-framed houses are protected from the elements by this method of walling.

The advantages of the material are good thermal insulation properties (far better than brickwork laid in one skin) and lightness in weight. The writer has surveyed many period timber-framed houses with wattle-and-daub walls and found the material to be in an excellent state of repair and condition. The best way to effect a repair is to employ first principles. All too often slightly defective panels are stripped out and replaced with lightweight concrete blocks, rendered and plastered. What is not thought about is that the weight of a concrete block, together with rendering and plaster, is considerably greater than the wattle-and-daub panel for which the frame was designed and unnecessary stresses and loadings may be imposed on the frame. The specification for the repair of daub may vary quite considerably throughout the country, but any daub mix should be as dry as possible so that shrinkage is kept to a minimum level. Some shrinkage will always occur and must be attended to in the repair process.

Limewash can be made by adding shredded tallow to lump lime which has been broken down. Water as hot as possible should be added, and after slaking, the consistency thinned to that of milk. Wherever possible follow the original ways, but it is generally acceptable to use slates wedged between close frame structures where these are present to give extra rigidity (see Fig 64). In larger square panels the use of galvanised or non-rusting alloy metal lathing is acceptable to serve the same purpose. Do not add cement to the mix as this will harden the compound, ruin the overall effect and shorten the life of the repair. Any clay used in alternative mixing should, if at all possible, be obtained locally, as the consistency is then more likely to be compatible. The job should with care be well within the realms of the DIY owner, provided the mix of the materials is consistent with that described. Any staining to the timber frame as a result of the repair work may be cleaned off using soap and water applied with a scrubbing brush.

Repairs to wattle-and-daub panels can also be made in non-traditional ways using modern materials and with thermal insulation in mind. Two methods are illustrated in Figs 66 and 67 (p117) and both have proved a success.

Method A Assuming the wattle-and-daub panel to be in a state whereby conventional or traditional repair is not practicable, the panel members should be removed in entirety to expose the structural frame on both horizontal and vertical faces. The frame members should be treated and made good as necessary ready to receive the new panel. Battens are fixed to the inside edges of the frame to form a square and, if the panel is large, intermediate battens should be fixed to strengthen or reinforce the new panel covering. The battens should be treated and the best available choice is probably tanalised wood. Tanalised battens are readily available in most builders' merchants or wood-yards and are only a little more expensive than normal battens. The writer would suggest that battens of size 50 × 25mm might be most appropriate. A wood-wool slab panel should be nailed to the battens on the outside face and, dependent upon the size of the repair, this can be in one or more pieces. A layer of 25mm thick fibreglass quilt should be laid against the inside of the wood-wool slab against a layer of building paper and cut to fit into the squares formed by the 50 × 25mm tanalised battens. This can be held in place by a skin of 500-gauge polythene sheet which is attached to the batten on the inside so that the fibreglass quilt is sandwiched. On the inside face, a sheet of 13mm insulation board should be cut and fixed to the battens to enclose the complete structure so far. Externally, the wood-wool slab is rendered with a mix of lime, cement and sand in the proportions of 1:1:6. Internally, the insulation board should be coated with plaster to a depth of about 3mm. The internal and external vertical and horizontal frame members are left exposed and can be cleaned off, treated and made good as necessary. The writer would recommend that, on the external face, a minimum recess of 9mm is left between the external face of rendering and the external face of oak frame-work. It is also highly recommended that a mastic joint is bedded onto the oak frame around the perimeter of the panel to avoid water ingress.

Method B This method is recommended by the Society for the Protection of Ancient Buildings and is appropriate if traditional repairs are not possible. The oak frame should be exposed, cleaned and made good as necessary. A mastic impregnated foam strip, ie Compriband, Fakband, etc, is compressed to the insides of the vertical and horizontal frame members with tanalised batten of size 50 × 25mm. The use of galvanised screws is recommended to avoid corrosion of the metal from tannic acid in the oak frame. A layer of expanded polystyrene insulation board should be placed over the battens and held in position with galvanised expanded metal lathing on both inside and outside faces. A polythene vapour barrier should be included between the polystyrene layer and the lathing on the inside face and a layer of breather type building paper between the polystyrene and lathing on the outside face. Lathing should be nailed to the tanalised battens with galvanised nails at appropriate centres. Externally, the galvanised lathing is rendered with a mix of cement lime and sharp sand in the proportions of 1:4:12. The completed render coat should be finished with three coats of limewash to avoid water ingress. A lead tray should be formed on the sills and rendering carried over this. It is important to coat the underside of the lead tray with paint to avoid tannic acid attack to the lead. Internally, the galvanised expanded metal lathing should be coated with lime plaster. It is recommended that a ledge of about 9mm be left between the inside face of the lime plaster and the inside face of the oak framing members. It is also important that the vapour barrier be thoroughly sealed around the edge of the internal face of the oak frame. Any cracks in the oak frame should not be filled with cement mortar as this will trap and retain any moisture present. The Society for the Protection of Ancient Buildings recommend the use of a mixture of fine oak sawdust and 'Unibond' adhesive mixed 1:1 by volume. A water-based wood stain can be used if necessary to achieve a colour match in the filling. The mixture should be tightly pressed into the crack or cavity and, when dry, can be treated or shaped as the surrounding wood.

TILE-HANGING

The weatherproofing of a period timber-framed house was always a problem, and in original form such buildings must have been uncomfortable with draughts and rain-water penetrating the structure in many different ways. Wall panels were perhaps the biggest problem, and from the end of the sixteenth century a great many older houses, and indeed the newer ones, were clad to give better protection from the elements. The two main types of applied claddings were tiles and timber boards, although the older method of plaster was still popular and remained so until the eighteenth century. As would be expected, cladding forms varied throughout the regions, and tile-hanging became common in and around Surrey, Kent and Sussex, and some parts of Hampshire and Berkshire. In Kent and other parts of Essex, timber cladding was more common. At first plain tiles were used, similar to those employed in roofs, although often a little thinner in section. Each tile was commonly hung to give a triple lap and the upper part was usually embedded in lime and hair mortar to form a watertight seal.

The tiles were usually fixed to horizontal battens by means of oak or hazel pegs but were sometimes nailed. A specially shaped tile was manufactured for corners. Slightly decorated tiles were sometimes used in association with plain tiles to form a pattern or design on the wall face. Kent, perhaps, has the best tile-hanging, and local clays produced the terracotta tiles commonly seen in the Weald area. Tile-hanging in Kent, Surrey and Sussex tends to favour plain tiles, although the patterned tile is also a common sight in Surrey. The elevation of a building clad in hand-made clay tiles is a delight, and when these are replaced with the later machine-made tiles the effect is totally lost. Normally, tile-hanging is restricted to the upper floors and gable ends of period timber-framed houses because these are usually the most exposed parts of the structure (see Fig 47, p71).

The mathematical tile, or brick tile as it is sometimes known, is a

128

more formal variety of tile-hanging which was designed to give a wall the general appearance of being constructed of brickwork. These were generally hung on horizontal battens or boards, and were usually nailed in place. They are commonly found in Kent and Sussex, but usually only in the more urban areas.

Tile-hanging can cause an owner much aggravation and expense owing to dampness. To remain in sound condition, tile-hung walls must be as watertight as possible, to which end use of lead flashing is immensely important. One of the most common defects in tile-hanging is the rotted tile batten which occurs because water has been allowed to penetrate freely the space between the back of the tile and the face of the structure. There are two main fixing methods: the first and by far the best is the hanging of vertical tiles to horizontal timber battens. These in turn are fixed to the vertical oak studs, often with iron nails. There are two problems with this detail: first, if the top edge of the tile-hanging is not properly flashed with lead, water will penetrate and eventually rot the horizontal battens, causing the tiles to become dislodged and fall. Water penetration will also inevitably rot any timber tile pegs, with the same result to the tile. The second problem is the method by which the horizontal battens are fixed to the vertical oak studs. We have already discussed the problems of metal fixings to oak (pp106–8) and the effects of tannic acid on metal (see pp 97–8). If iron nails have been used as a method of fixing, the joint effects of dampness and tannic-acid attack will certainly destroy the connections of the batten with the timber frame. Where vertical tile-hanging needs repair and battening has been used, the replacement battens must be tanalised or treated in some other suitable way against the destructive effects of dampness, rot and insect attack.

Suitably treated battens should be fixed to the oak frame with tannic acid-resisting screws. Brass is very suitable for this purpose. If the tiles are of a nib type, they can be hung directly on to the top edge of the tile battens; if they are of a peg type, it is vitally important to ensure that the pegs used are made of a suitable alloy, are galvanised or of copper. The copper peg is likely to be extremely expensive, but local builder's merchants often carry, or can order, suitable galvanised or composition nails, one variety of which is short and stubby and is designed especially for tile-hanging.

It is a good practice to hang vertical tiles from suitably treated battening because the method allows a free flow of air all around the tile, thus helping to eliminate dry-rot, the greatest of all problems. A 4lb (1.8kg) lead flashing to the underside of eaves and around any

129

structural opening in the tile-hung wall should not be forgotten.

The second, but less commonly used, method of fixing vertical tile-hanging is by direct nailing through the tile and into the substructural wall without the use of battening. The fixing may be made into oak framing, horizontal lime mortar in a brick panel or a rendered wall. The obvious defect is of water penetration and the effect on a rusty iron nail which suddenly breaks, allowing the tile to fall. This method should be avoided at all costs as it actively encourages dry-rot in the external wall frame owing to a lack of air circulation. It also allows water to build up in the enclosed area behind the tile, thus causing penetrating dampness to the structural frame and sub-structural wall panels beneath the tiling.

When repairs are carried out to vertical tile-hanging, the lap between the tile courses should be about 1½in (3.8cm) but in certain circumstances the degree of lap can be less. It should be remembered that there are three courses of tile at any point of lap. The ideal arrangement is a counter batten of 2 × 1in (5 × 2.5cm) treated soft-wood fixed at 15in (37.5cm) centres vertically upon which horizontal battens can be fixed. The ideal is not always possible because the new work must match the projection from the wall of the original work which could be substantially less. It is not absolutely necessary when vertical tile-hanging to fix a sheet of vertical bituminous felt behind the battens as the tiles, if properly hung, should afford enough protection to the substructural wall. If, however, the wall in question is in a particularly exposed position, the use of a bituminous felt layer nailed behind the battens might be considered. The argument against this is that the bituminous layer of felt can also hold penetrating moisture between the inside layer and the outside of the substructural face to which it is attached.

As a general point, never use machine-made clay tiles as hanging on a period timber-framed house. They are constructionally incorrect and aesthetically disastrous. They do have a place in building, but not in connection with this type of property.

WEATHER-BOARDING

The tile is arguably the best form of cladding, but the cheapest is certainly the horizontal weather-board or clapboard. It was commonly used in preference to tiling when economy was a major concern and it is therefore found principally on smaller buildings.

Weather-boarding was probably first used on farm buildings, especially barns in the early seventeenth century. It became a common cladding material during the eighteenth century on the domestic timber-framed house. Early weather-boarding was superior in that it was formed of oak or elm and pegged to the structural timber frame. In later development it was commonly softwood, fixed directly to the structural posts and beams. Each board lapped the one below with a vertical strip joined to the side returns of the doors and windows to create an end stop for the horizontal boards to butt against. The earlier oak and elm boarding was commonly left untreated, but in exposed coastal areas it was sometimes painted with black tar. Tar painting, which is an inferior type of cladding, was also used on later softwood. The boards may be laid using a feather-edge arrangement whereby the top edge is feathered and covered by the lower and thicker edge of the board above (see Plate 22 p74).

Alternatively, shiplap cladding may be used with the relatively modern tongue-and-groove construction. When restoring clapboard walls, an owner should always try to match new material with the old. If oak or elm boarding was adopted on the original structure, every effort should be made to match it. Do not, under any circumstances, mix new softwood or other types of hardwood with the original boarding as this will have disastrous effects. If the weatherboarding has a painted finish, the decorations must be kept in a good state of repair. Any rotted timber should be removed and replaced with timber of a similar size, section and thickness. New wood should be thoroughly primed, undercoated and topcoated with a suitable paint, taking into account the amount of weathering the wall is likely to endure.

ROOF TIMBERS AND JOINTS

The medieval carpenter rarely used anything but oak pegs or trenails to secure the joints made in both wall and roof timbers. The pegs were cut from heart of oak and, when maintained, are as good today as when they were first fixed. Metal fixings were possible but too expensive and the effect of tannic acid on iron was known for all its dangers. When metal work is observed in a medieval building in the form of brackets or clamps, it can be safely assumed that it is of a more recent addition, perhaps an attempt to repair a burst joint or a dislodged member in the frame. It has been established that the

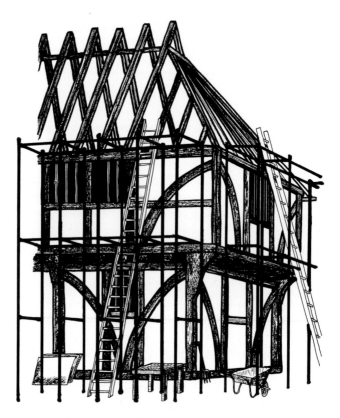

Fig 69 **Restoration works to an open hall house in west Sussex.** This example is in the process of being re-roofed.

medieval carpenter was familiar with the mortice and tenon, lap-dovetail and range of scarf joints, and that his technical ability is to be admired today. After about 1600, softwood was introduced into timber-frame building and so was iron, causing a decline in the previously high standard of carpentry. Much later joints were formed using iron plates and bolts, but this period is not to be discussed in these pages.

Restoration of period timber-framed roofs is a difficult subject and there are various opinions and ideals as to how it should be done. There is much to be said for repairing oak with oak and indeed this point has already been made under the section on wall frames (see p102). The skilful modern carpenter assures us that any repair can be carried out using oak in the manner of the old masters. Unfortunately, the supply of suitably skilled carpenters today is not what it used to be, and costs are proportionately high. The use of plastics in

132

repair is favourable in this respect. Concern today is to preserve as much as possible of the old work, which is an admirable philosophy, but historically, if a building fell into disrepair, it would have been pulled down without a second thought. That is one reason why there are so many surviving timber buildings with second-hand timber in the roofs and walls. An individual member found to be seriously defective would have been renewed in its entirety and not patch repaired as we do today.

In some schools of thought it is preferable to use suitably treated metal to effect a repair rather than attempt the difficult patching or replacing of a timber structural member. For instance, in medieval days, a cracked collar would have been taken out and replaced with a new member. Today, the collar could be removed and replaced, but the original timber would then be lost from the building. The use of specialist bolts and straps can effect a repair and at the same time maintain the original character of the existing timber. In any event, the repair should be as unobtrusive as practically possible and metal work hidden from view wherever possible (see Figs 65, 78–9).

One roof timber likely to be affected by rot because of leaking roofs and gutters is the wall plate. Worse still, dry-rot is the most likely variety. In the event of a wall-plate section having to be replaced, a new section of timber can be spliced in using a longitudinal bevelled dovetail halving joint or an edge-halved scarf (see Fig 12, p26). A wall plate carries the feet of rafters and is a rigid member which should not be weakened by cutting or poor jointing. The same applies to sill beams as they are equally rigid members of the structural frame.

Common rafters often need replacement owing to rot or insect attack; the original timber should be saved wherever possible. Where a joint can be made above a purlin, the scarf is perhaps the best connection to use (see Figs 12–17, pp26–8, and Plate 35). Timbers held in compression, including principal rafters and struts, can also be scarfed together using the stop splayed with under-squinted square butt and transverse key joint (see Fig 13, p26). Timbers subject to bending stress, such as beams and purlins, can also be scarfed with this joint. The new timber must be of a similar quality, section and grain to make the joint a success.

In making a joint between new and old oak, the saw cuts must be as close as possible to a right angle to avoid the wood splitting and a stepped joint adopted to ensure an accurate fit. The DoE accepts the use of oak pegs to hold a joint together, but asks for waterproof glue

Plate 35 **Roof repairs.** A repair to a rafter using new oak.

to be used to give extra strength.

Knots in timbers under tension, together with saw cuts, slots, holes and mortices, can cause structural failure. A longitudinal defect such as a shake is not so much of a problem. The strength of a beam under tension is largely dependent upon the continuity of the grain, and therefore great attention should be paid to this when notching in beams. Such defective members may be a tie-beam or collar, a brace or a bressummer. In these cases the use of a plated scarf joint to effect a repair is usual, but the plating must be hidden from view. It is recommended, however, that any person undertaking such repairs should seek expert advice beforehand.

It may be possible to repair a tie-beam which has only a relatively low loading but which is under tension by cutting out the defective area of wood and replacing it with new wood of similar type, scale and section using a suitably pegged mortice-and-tenon joint at either end. Alternatively, a steel flitch plate (see Fig 78 p158) may be used. The structural mechanics of this repair are outside the scope of this book, but a restorer should call in a structural engineer to advise on such defects.

A common defect is in the beam which has fractured along its length, as distinct from extensively rotted, the likely cause being the subjection of the beam to a bending stress. Such a defect can be repaired by the use of a steel plate inserted in a slot cut along the bottom edge of the member, this having the effect of reinstating the tensile strength of the beam (see Figs 78–9). Damage of a lesser extent but for the same basic reason can be repaired by providing a steel tension strap anchored to sound timber in the beam, or stressed by bolts passing into sound timber on either side of the offending fracture. This repair is most suited to the early roof and can be used, for instance, where crown-post construction has been adopted (see Plates 24–6, p80).

In carrying out any repairs to oak roofs incorporating steel as reinforcement, the restorer should be mindful of the effects of tannic acid on the metal. Only stainless steel should be used for such repairs. Most importantly, sill beams and wall plates rely on complicated halving joints and bevelled and dovetailed lengthening joints to avoid the effects of outward buckling as a result of thrust from inadequately tied rafters. Any attempt at repair or restoration of these members should be mindful of the mechanical forces upon them and the medieval details should be followed as closely as possible to ensure adequacy.

Joints in members at the apex and eaves of a roof structure are particularly likely to be affected by rot and insect attack. Other joints are likely to be affected by these elements, but are more likely to fail as a result of movement in the structural timber frame. Any repair to a joint must be carried out in a manner which will enable the joint to perform in the context for which it was designed, and this often entails the removal and replacement of damaged timber by another in precisely the same form. It is possible to repair a partly rotted joint and to piece in timber to complete the job, or to use plastics as shown in Fig 68, p118.

A rotten tenon can be cut off, a new one formed and connected to the mortice and the whole assembly then pegged back into place. The false tenon may require extra room for positioning in the mortice, in which case an extra deep mortice should be cut in the old timber to allow the false tenon to slide into position and to be wedged tight. A mortice can be similarly repaired by reinstating beams and posts with new wood, bonded with waterproof glue. Using these methods, the joint between collar and rafters, tie-beams and wall plates, purlins and principal rafters can be restored. In repairing a joint, the connection between the members of the frame must have an amount of flexibility to allow seasonal and natural movement. The mortice and tenon is a slotted joint and can therefore allow such natural movements. Oak beams should never be bolted to wall plates or connected without some factor of tolerance being taken into account. Failure to do so could produce the result described in the house in Hampshire which all but collapsed as a result of roof spread. Distortion of the oak frame is common, often because green oak was used by the

Plate 36 (above left) **Roof repairs.** Repair of a rafter foot and a recent section of wall plate.

Plate 37 (above right) **Roof repairs.** Restored wall plate, tie-beam and rafter. Note the matching timber and grain.

Plate 38 (below left) **Roof repairs.** A corner roof repair using matching oak and typical joints.

Plate 39 (below right) **Roof repairs.** See Plate 38.

medieval builder. Natural distortion is not a problem and gives character to the period timber-framed house. Defects in the joints, however, are a serious problem and must be corrected to ensure the structural stability of the frame.

The ends of rafters and ceiling joists are prone to rot, more often than not as a result of leaking rain-water gutters (see Plates 36–42). In this case the use of a metal or wood connector is acceptable where necessary to provide a better connection with masonry structure (see Figs 78–80). Quite adequate on smaller timbers is a joint formed by cutting off the ends of the defective scantling and lapping in a new section with bolts and connectors. The split-ring type of connector, designed to join timber to timber, is preferred if this method is to be adopted. A split purlin may require an additional strut inserted at the point of failure, wedged into place sufficiently to prevent further structural movement but not so as to cause upward thrust in the roof. A damaged strut can be left in place and a new one of similar section inserted next to it to add reinforcement.

Tile battens are commonly defective on hand-made clay-tiled roofs as a result of surface water leaking through the tiles and into the timber members. When tiles are removed from the roof, the old defective battening should be stripped off to expose principal and common rafters. In the writer's opinion, waterproof sarking felt should not be placed over an oak roof because it should be left to breathe naturally, although this is a matter of personal preference. What is vital, however, is to properly treat tile battens as a precaution against rot in the event of any future leakage and the effects of fungal and wood-boring insect attack. Most builders' merchants carry stocks of green tanalised tile batten which serve the purpose adequately.

As a general point, when a roof is stripped, it is an ideal time to ask a timber infestation company to spray the roof timbers to protect them against rot and insect attack; it is also an ideal opportunity to clean the roof timbers and exposed roof void. The infestation company should be able to provide a twenty- or thirty-year guarantee for their work, and this should be kept with the deeds and associated documents to pass on to a new owner.

ROOF COVERINGS

Roof construction is directly related to wall frames and panels. In box frame construction, the roof frame is a separate structural member from the external wall frame. It would be able to stand whether or not it were attached. In cruck construction, roofs and walls are one integral structure unit.

Plate 40 (left) **Roof repairs.** Repair to a hipped end incorporating a jack rafter.
Plate 41 (centre) **Roof repairs.** Repairs to a wall plate and rafters. The hip is also restored using new oak.
Plate 42 (right) **Roof repairs.** A view in the carpenters' yard of restored rafters and wall plate.

To a large extent the material of the outer roof covering determines the shape and pitch of the roofs and the construction method. To simplify roof construction, features such as valleys, hips and dormers tend not to appear on roofs designed for slate covering. All of these do, however, occur on roofs designed for thatch and hand-made clay tiles. The style of the roof also has a bearing on the pitch, and there is a direct relationship between the steepness of the pitch 'and the amount of work in it. The tendency is for more elaborate roofs to be the steepest in pitch, thus shedding surface water in a more efficient manner and avoiding ingress of water to inner parts of the building. Local traditions also influenced the roof shape and coverings, as did the availability of local materials. The Wealden houses of Sussex and Kent had very large roofs, quite steeply pitched and covered with clay tiles. In Surrey the tiled and hipped roof was common, whereas in eastern counties the gabled roof is more common. In the Cotswolds a predominant feature was the dormer, formed by building the main external wall up to form a small gable. The roof of the dormer was almost as high as the building and many houses were built with several dormers in a row as a feature. This method of construction, however, was unsuitable with the timber frame and such houses were usually stone built. Houses of the fifteenth and sixteenth centuries can readily be seen with thatched roofs as well as clay-tile coverings. Examples of thatch on seventeenth-century framed houses can be found in most areas.

Tiles were used on the roofs of box-framed houses in three south-eastern counties in the seventeenth century, and thatch in profusion on both eastern and western buildings. Originally, reed thatch was restricted to the Fens and Broads of East Anglia but now, of course, with better transportation, roofs covered in this material can be seen all over the country. In Norfolk and Suffolk wheat-straw thatch can still be seen.

Thatch The Old English word for any roof covering was 'thack'. In early days roofs were covered with straw, reed, heather, variations of these materials and anything else of a vegetable matter that grew locally. As a result, early roofs were said to have 'thack' coverings and the direct derivation of this term is 'thatch', now limited to a particular type of roof covering. Until the seventeenth century, thatch was probably the most widespread form of roof covering in Europe and continued as such for many years. Often large and important buildings were roofed in this material, including churches, particularly in East Anglia. Ideally, for financial reasons the covering was suitable for small buildings because the materials were readily and locally available and, of course, inexpensive. Also, a poor quality roof constructed of inferior scantlings could support the relatively light weight of the covering.

Rain-water disposal methods with thatch are simple as no gutters or down-pipes are required. Fire, however, was perhaps the major hazard and in some parts, especially London, it was compulsory to give the covering a coat of limewash to protect it from sparks. In London thatch became illegal on safety grounds and other major cities followed suit. It did, however, survive in rural areas where straw and reed were plentiful and cheap, such as Norfolk, Suffolk, Essex, Cambridge and parts of Dorset. In areas of Devon the covering is used on buildings whose cob walls are not strong enough to take other alternative materials. Fire, of course, is still a major problem with thatched roofs and long summer droughts can, and often do, have disastrous results on buildings covered with this material (see Appendix 3). There are still skilled thatchers in existence but, because the practice of thatching has declined, the numbers have diminished to an alarming degree. It is now possible to treat thatched roofs with a fire-retardant additive, but the dangers still exist.

A thatched roof is liable to need patch repair around ridges and

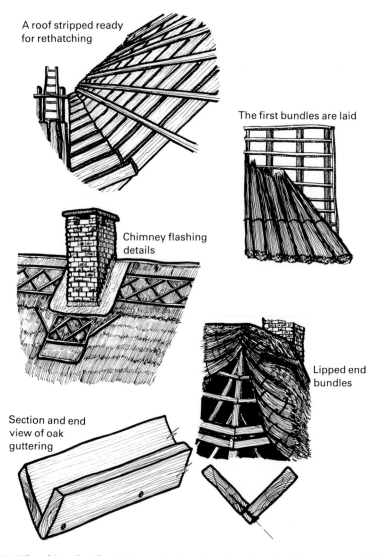

A roof stripped ready for rethatching

The first bundles are laid

Chimney flashing details

Lipped end bundles

Section and end view of oak guttering

Fig 70 **Thatching details.** Various sketches showing the thatching process. Ridges and roof planes are often decorated.

valleys long before it is necessary to replace the entire covering. The defective parts can be covered with netting to stop birds and vermin entering and causing more damage. When a portion is to be renewed, it is common to strip back the dilapidated area and lay the new thatch, starting at the base of the stripped area. In its stripped form the substructure is likely to consist of timber battens laid at about 8in (20cm) centres. A yealm of thatch, being about 6in (15cm) deep and

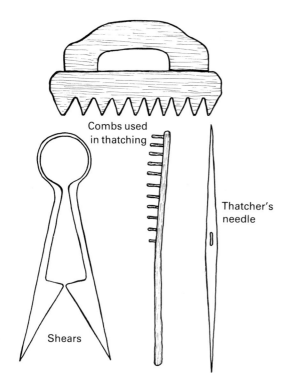

Combs used in thatching

Thatcher's needle

Shears

Fig 71 **Thatching tools.** Some typical thatchers' tools.

10in (2.5cm) wide, is tied at the butt with twine and laid upon the roof. It is then tied to the battens or fixed with withies nailed to the common rafters. Each lap of the layer of yealm should be 50 per cent covered. Further layers of yealms are then fastened by rods laid across them and these are bound to the rafters with twine. Usually the twine is treated with tar to extend its life. Once the bared area is covered, it is raked down with a timber rake designed specifically for the purpose and the edges trimmed with a pair of shears (see Figs 70–1). On the ridge the yealm is bent over and coated with slaked lime and earth. The ends of the top yealm on the other side of the roof are then pressed down into the mix of slaked lime and earth and the whole area is weighted with a further coat. The ridge is then capped with thatch and laced with withies to the roof.

The eaves and verges are also laced with withies in a similar manner. Whenever it is necessary to repair thatch, the restorer should consult a surveyor or architect with an understanding of the principles involved so that he might check the old rafters for structural strength and suitability for recovering. The professional thatcher, for his part, is quite likely to expect the restorer to have the rafters checked out by a surveyor. It is unreasonable to expect him to take responsibility for the failure of a newly thatched roof because of structural failure in the roof members.

For centuries the most common of thatching materials was ordinary straw, often left over after the harvesting of wheat, rye, barley and oats. This type of straw is often known in thatching as 'long straw'. Wheat straw was perhaps the most commonly used, but rye was the favourite. Oat and barley straw were normally used only if the other two varieties were not at hand. Wheat straw for thatching purposes is best harvested when still green, in which state it is not brittle and is more economic to handle. The winter crop is generally the best, but long straw is unfortunately harder to obtain than it used to be. Combine harvesters and mechanical balers break up the material, rendering it useless for thatching purposes. The best thatching straw is a winter crop cut by the old methods and collected without breaking the stalks.

In thatching areas it will be found that certain farmers raise a good income out of parcels of land set aside specifically for thatching long straw which the thatcher may be able to harvest himself, thus cutting overhead costs. Long straw is laid in a lengthwise fashion, similar to layers of hair on a head, and the eaves and barges are finished with long runners. Unfortunately, long straw is not a highly durable thatch and a roof covered in it would require total replacement long before one covered in Norfolk reed or Devon wheat reed thatch.

Norfolk reed grows best in salt water and is found in the marshy estuaries and broads of Norfolk. It is a tall grower, can achieve lengths of up to about 8ft (2.4m) and can only be harvested after a heavy frost has killed the 'flags' or leaves on the stems. The Norfolk reed is usually cut after December and harvested throughout the winter months. A regular harvest is essential to ensure continuance of the cherished long straight stem. There are now mechanical means of cutting Norfolk reed and it is usually tied up into bundles of about 1ft (30cm) in diameter and stacked in piles of six, known in the trade as fathoms. Norfolk reed is laid so that the sharp ends of the stalk are exposed and point outwards, thus shedding surface water from end to end down the roof plane.

At the beginning of the nineteenth century straw roofs in Devon were combed with a metal comb to produce a clean, aligned stem known as combed wheat reed or Devon reed. This material was laid in a similar fashion to Norfolk reed with the ends of the straw exposed. Modern wheat is not suitable for this process, and in thatching areas special crops are grown for the purpose. There are still examples of other thatching materials in use and these include heather and sedge. Heather was once commonly used in non-wheat or reed-growing areas such as the north-east of England, Scotland and in the Westcountry, on Dartmoor for instance. The heather was commonly cut in the autumn while in bloom and laid with the roots pointed outwards. After a time the outer surface turns black, which is not very attractive, but can still be seen in parts of Scotland.

Sedge is commonly used to ridge the Norfolk reed roof and in the Fens can be seen as an entire roofing cover. Thatching spars are commonly made of hazel and come in two main types: the sway is a long rod, about 1in (2.5cm) wide and is used to hold down the thatch; the staple is much shorter, about ½in (1.25cm) wide, and is used to secure the ridge or, in long straw roofs, the barges and eaves or gables. The contemporary thatcher may have his own hazel coppice, but many are now resorting to the use of tempered steel sways. These replace the old hazel sways which are commonly attacked by wood-boring insects. Hazel, however, is still used to make spars and liggers (see Fig 70, p140).

Long straw thatch is the cheapest to lay but is also the shortest lived. Norfolk reed is by far the most durable but also comparatively expensive. The typical life-span of thatched coverings is difficult to estimate, but assuming the varieties are laid to a good and equal standard, are maintained and not subjected to extremely wet conditions, long straw should last for between ten and twenty years, combed wheat reed for about twenty to forty years and Norfolk reed from about fifty to seventy years. It is likely that some roofs covered in Norfolk reed have not been renewed after less than a hundred years, but all will require regular maintenance and perhaps patching at intervals during their life.

The dangers of fire and other hazards of thatched roofs have been mentioned (see Appendix 3). Insurance companies are familiar with the problems and are likely to charge up to five times the premium on a thatched roof to cover the dangers. It is now possible to soak the thatched roof in a fire-retardant fluid which can be applied to a completed roof, although not very successfully; as the fluid must penetrate the thatch very thoroughly, it is far better applied to the bundles before they are laid on the roof structure. A thatched roof provides good insulation in both winter and summer and is also an effective sound-proofing material. The covering is ideally suited to the period timber-framed house and provides excellent all-round protection from the elements.

The covering may require repair, however, and if this is the case it is always a good idea to find out who thatched the building last or who carried out the most recent repairs. This thatcher may know the building well and be aware of any problems peculiar to the particular thatch. A prospective owner should be aware that thatch is expensive and that a total replacement job, even on the smallest of roofs, is likely to cost several thousands of pounds. There may even be a case for considering change of the outer roof covering from thatch to tile or some other appropriate local material. If the building is listed, then any material change to the appearance will require listed building consent. In the writer's experience, local authorities are reluctant to grant this to anyone, but a person who buys a property and then wishes to change its appearance on economic grounds is not likely to be granted permission. Local authorities are also extremely reluctant to change thatched roof coverings for other types in areas where thatch is a local tradition or where a building forms part of a group which are thatched.

In carrying out rethatching work it is not always essential to strip thoroughly all the old roof covering. Many thatchers would be reluctant to do this and would most certainly advise on necessity. A good thatcher is likely to suggest laying a fire-resistant barrier between new thatch and rafters, and of the many types available the thatcher is likely to have his own preferences. Such a barrier also helps to keep a roof void clear of thatching debris which must be expected on roofs of this type.

The thatcher is also likely to have specific views on the question of wiring the outside face. It is true that birds can cause havoc in a thatched roof, especially one covered in wheat reed or long straw. Vermin are also a problem in some areas, although to an extent wiring will not keep them out. The use of wire is often criticised as being ugly and unnatural and a further argument is that it tends to restrict the natural down-flow of surface water from the roof. This in turn can lead to a build-up of moss on the outside face which is damaging and unsightly on a thatched roof. The writer had a friend with a thatched roof and one day an electrical fire started which totally destroyed the house. The Fire Brigade said that they could probably have saved a large portion of the building if they could have pulled the thatch off the roof. The thatch was held in place, however, with wire and the building was totally destroyed. Any thatcher who uses wire as a protective outside covering is likely to say that he will fix the wire in such a way that it can be pulled off the roof with relative ease. It may not always be best, however, to remove the thatch in the event of fire and one argument in favour of wire is that removal of the outside coverings only causes extra through-draught in the burning building, thus making the fire more efficient (see Appendix 3).

Very few thatched roofs have rain-water gutters and down-pipes. A likely problem that occurs if the eaves overhang is minimal is water penetration from the roof to timber-framed wall panels. As a result of water ingress by this method, rot is likely to occur to framing members and joints. Traditionally, a thatched roof with minimal overhang was fitted with timber gutters as shown in Fig 70. Rethatching of a roof does not require Building Regulations consent, but it may be politic to advise the planning office of proposals if, for no other reason, to update their records. A new thatched roof cannot be constructed within 13yd (12m) of a site boundary. While this does not affect rethatching, it does affect any matching extensions which an owner may be considering adding to his house. The regulation also applies to a building which may have been tiled or covered with some other material but upon which the owner wishes to place thatch perhaps to match other existing buildings in the immediate area. One other important point on the positive side is that local authorities have the power to relax Building Regulations if they feel the need is appropriate, but this is largely a question for negotiation in individual cases.

Hand-made clay plain tiles Hand-made clay plain tiles have a history dating back to the Roman period. The Romans used clay tiles for roofing purposes and their bricks and pavings were made of a similar material, which was not very different in appearance from the roofing tile. When the Romans left Britain, the roofing tile left with them, but the ordinance of 1212 required new roofs in towns to be covered with materials other than thatch. The ordinance gave the clay tile a clean bill of health and recommended it as a suitable roofing material in city areas. After 1300 small houses had tiled roofs, although there was not a standard size as such and quality was not consistent. A statute of 1477 laid down certain criteria for the preparation of the clay used, and also standardised the size of the tile at approximately 10in (26.25cm) × 6¼in (15.6cm) × ⅝in (1.5cm) thick. Local differences persisted and tiles still varied in size, partly dependent upon quantity and heat in the kiln fire. In 1725 George I laid down fresh standards and an average tile was reduced slightly to a size of 9½in (23.7cm) × 5¾in (14.3cm) × ½in (1.25cm) thick.

Early hand-made clay tiles were laid without soakers and flashings. At junctions with vertical surfaces, a water fillet was used. There are, of course, many old and somewhat neglected roofs in existence where this detail can still be found. The surveyor should be in a position to point out such defects when he does his structural survey of the building.

Many hand-made clay tiles fail as the result of uneven consistency in the clay mix and uneven burning in the kilns. Even so, a high proportion of such tiles are tough and durable and survive today on roofs all over the country. Typically, they have a rough and textured outer surface with characteristic irregularities in both size and sectional shape. Often they are coated with areas of relatively harmless lichen which seem attracted to the clay and have great aesthetic appeal. The camber from top to bottom of the tile is designed to stop water seepage under the tile, but they usually have a cross camber which tends to allow water to seep under the edges. Tiles are commonly hung on two oak or hazel pegs placed over the edge of a rent oak lath (see Glossary of Terms). The type of lath most commonly seen today is fir or pine, and is of much later date. The nail was not used as a fixing for hand-made clay roof tiles and they often remained on a roof held down largely by their own weight but with some fixings provided by pegs.

Rafters were set in pairs connected at the top without a ridge and battens were merely laid across the rafters at right angles. This allowed the tiles to be inspected from the underside, this being an exposed face inside the building. It is often a surprise to see the outside tile coverings in apparently sound condition with all tiles acceptably in line. This takes into account the rickety appearance of some old roofs on timber-framed buildings which have moved somewhat over the years. The real surprise comes when the inside face of a tile is viewed and it is found that the timber pegs have rotted, leaving the tiles seemingly unsupported. Tile pegs usually rot as a result of moisture penetration through the outer clay-tile coverings, but they are also commonly attacked by wood-boring insects. Normally, the hand-made clay-tiled roof has a pitch in excess of 45° and many are in excess of 52°, being the minimum necessary for older, but now discarded, thatched coverings. Clay tiles should have a lap of at least 2½in (6.25cm) to be effective in this respect, although in practice many roofs are standing and relatively water-

146

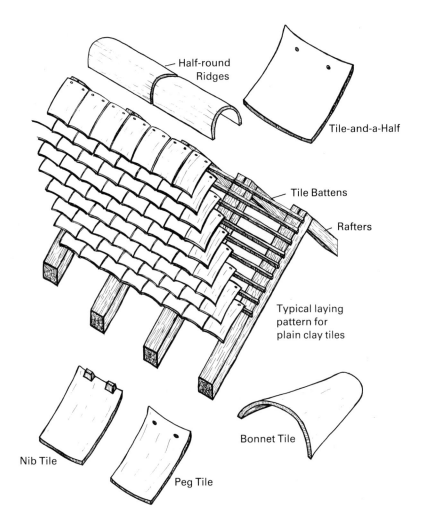

Half-round Ridges

Tile-and-a-Half

Tile Battens

Rafters

Typical laying pattern for plain clay tiles

Nib Tile

Peg Tile

Bonnet Tile

Fig 72 **Plain clay tile roof details.** This sketch shows a roof partially tile covered and types of tile in common usage.

tight with less than the normal standard of cover.

When the surveyor inspects a house, it is vital that he is able to gain access to the roof void to inspect the underside of any clay-tile coverings. He must view the method and condition of tile fixings and also look at the condition of tile battens and connections to the rafters. Most roofs have access hatches somewhere at first-floor ceiling level, although they are not always obvious. The writer has, on many occasions, had to squeeze into an airing- or clothes-cupboard because that is where the owner, or perhaps the previous occupier, had seen fit to place the only access point to the roof void. Woebetide the stocky surveyor who is physically unable to make the often perilous journey through sheets and blankets to that dark world above, often inhabited by bats, squirrels and vermin.

The collapsible aluminium ladder is a vital piece of equipment for the surveyor, but if a hatch is not provided in any form, one should be cut, ideally over a landing where access is liable to be easier. The surveyor who omits a roof void inspection may delude his client, who may well have a case in law against him for neglect.

It is common where double clay-tiled roofs occur for the outer roof planes to be in better condition than the inner. This is because access to the outer planes is easier and maintenance may have been carried out on a more regular basis. Attention must always be paid to connections of clay tiles with brickwork around chimney stacks. Tiles in this area will often be damaged because of movement in the structure, but also because various builders and owners have gained access to the stack for the purpose of repointing or chimney sweeping. We have discussed the effects of tannic acid on metalwork (see p 107) and this can be a problem at roof level. Tile battens are most likely to be fixed to rafters with common iron nails. Often, the battens or laths will be found to have sagged away from the fixing points at the rafter because of decay in the nail or natural movement in the main timber frame. Such movement can cause stress resulting

Fig 73 **A box-frame cottage in Hampshire.** A small box-frame cottage with tiled roof and wattle and daub infill panels.

148

Plate 43 **Roof repairs.** A roof in the process of being retiled with hand-made clay tiles.

in damage to clay tiles. Commonly, the eaves on an early hand-made clay-tile roof are left ragged and the undercloaking loose (see Fig 72 and Plate 43). Sections may be found missing or, more seriously, defective, and verges may show similar defects.

Valley details must always be given a close inspection, as any movement in the flat tiles will be manifest at the valley connections. Most clay-tiled roofs are capped with half-round clay-tile ridges. There are regional variations but the principle is the same. Any movement in the timber substructure or outer roof coverings will cause the ridges to become loose. Water penetration through the ridges is a common defect and can contribute to fungal and insect attack in the roof void. Structural roof timbers must be allowed to breathe and adequate ventilation of the roof void is essential. Whether this is by means of air-bricks, breather spaces or non-felting of the inner roof planes, is a matter of choice and specification.

Having assessed the general condition of a roof, it may be decided that only a few tiles need to be replaced. It is usually possible to find small quantities of tiles advertised for sale in local newspapers or on notice-boards. Often they are left over from a reroofing job and may be relatively inexpensive to buy. If, however, a large number of tiles are found to be defective, it is probably best to strip the entire roof and remove not only the defective tiles but also machine-made and concrete tiles which may have been inserted in previous repairs.

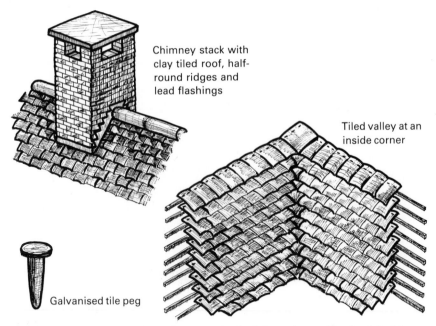

Chimney stack with clay tiled roof, half-round ridges and lead flashings

Tiled valley at an inside corner

Galvanised tile peg

Fig 74 **Chimney and roof details.** Water is shed from the roof by lead flashing or tiled valleys.

When reroofing a period timber-framed house it is vitally important to use only hand-made clay tiles and fixings and not cheaper machine-made alternatives. Machine-made tiles look wrong on a timber-framed house and have none of the appeal of a hand-made tile. It could also be said that manufacturers of hand-made clay tiles are few and far between. In order that our heritage is protected, we should encourage such manufacturers to stay in business and provide us with the correct materials for restoration purposes. When laying clay tiles, it is important to follow the lines of the old roof structure so that the original effect is not lost. Any levelling or firring of the structure should be kept to an absolute minimum as a 'squared-off' roof on a period timber-framed building not only looks wrong, it is wrong.

Whether or not waterproof sarking felt is used is a matter of opinion. The writer prefers not to use it in an old oak roof as air circulation is reduced when it is present. If pegs are being used to secure peg tiles to timber laths, felt will be found an inconvenience as the pegs are likely to interfere with the outer surface of felt. If nib tiles are used on sawn softwood battens, the felt will not interfere and may be an advantage. Alternatively, large headed nails may be used to fix peg tiles to sawn battens and the use of felt will not impede this detail. Any nails used should be galvanised for protection or preferably copper. Some alloy nails may be suitable in this respect. As a general rule, any battens used should be tanalised or treated with preservative fluid against rot and insect attack.

Ridge tiles, whether of hog-back or half-round pattern, should be matched with those on the original roof. All too often odd ridges are seen on a roof because it was too much trouble for an owner to find matching tiles. It is also true that in some areas, spare tiles are not easily found and in others there appears a glut of second-hand builders' merchants all selling spare parts at hugely inflated prices. Eaves tiles should be laid with a double course of tiles to give a traditional-looking tilt. Half-tiles should be used at verges to maintain a satisfactory tile bond and if a bargeboard was adopted, this should be carefully restored as a feature of the period timber-framed building (see Fig 72).

Valleys are probably best 'laced' at the corner using tiles and tiles-and-a-half to create the necessary bond (see Figs 72, 74). Hips are best finished with bonnet tiles as shown in Fig 72 and these bedded in mortar. Adequate flashings and soakers should be provided around chimney stacks and vertical abutments adjacent to pitched roof coverings. The writer prefers the use of lead as a flashing or alternatively a splayed-tile fillet as in Fig 74. The use of sand cement mortar as a fillet is common, but this fails with natural movement in the roof structure and water can then penetrate the roof via cracks formed.

CEILING JOISTS

Ceiling joists are often hidden from view. Where this occurs, repair can be made by simply doubling up the member with another of roughly the same size. The two members are best bolted together to provide a strong joint. If the defective timber is not rotted, it may be possible to bolt on a small section of new wood to provide local support in the affected area. If a defective section must be removed, any existing wood remaining should be properly and generously lapped to the new member to provide an adequate joint.

In a period timber-framed house the joist ends may be affected by rot as a result of leaking wall panels and water ingress. If a traditional repair is required, then a new section of joist may be scarfed onto the old and a new mortice and tenon formed at the external bressummer connection. Such a repair may not be possible or practical, however, in which case the use of timber connectors may be considered. Alternatively, a system of straps and bolts as illustrated in Figs 65, 68, 78–9 and 80 may be appropriate.

If a ceiling joist is split and it is not possible to remove an area of ceiling or adjacent structure, a repair can be made using flitch plates attached to either side of the joist and bolted through to each other (see Fig 78, p158). If additional strength is required, then shear plate connectors can be used. As an alternative, a duplicate section of timber can be bolted to the side using split ring connectors to make a fixing. Either way, the duplicate timber or plate must be of sufficient length to provide a stiff joint with any existing but sound timber beyond the split. It is strongly recommended that at least three bolts are used on either side of the defective portion to complete the repair.

Other repairs to ceiling joists can be carried out using the methods discussed in the section on suspended floors (see pp106–7, Figs 65, 68, 78–82 and the section dealing with metal and plastic repairs, pp 116–22).

SUSPENDED TIMBER FLOORS AT UPPER LEVEL

Suspended upper floors suffer from two main defects, both of which are common causes of alarm to house owners: sagging and excessive vibration. First, it is most important to ascertain the cause of the defect; nothing positive can be done to solve the problem until the exact cause is known. Sagging can cause the floor to tilt in any direction, thus making it difficult to stand furniture and effects. The writer's own house had settled towards the gable end by about 6in (15cm) over the length of the building. A heavily moulded oak trimmer ran the length of the building and first-floor joists were connected to it, forming the upper bedroom floors. At the gable end were two bedrooms over a study and a dining-room. When a person stood in the study and faced the rear of the house, the whole ceiling structure sloped alarmingly towards the left-hand side and created a strange optical illusion. The moulded trimmer was connected to a substantial oak post on the gable end which also leaned outwards owing to settlement over several centuries. The result of this was that the bed, chest of drawers and other items of furniture in one bedroom had to stand on chocks of varying thickness in order to compensate for the dramatic fall in the oak floor. The slope in the other bedroom was not so acute, but an amount of chocking was necessary to provide a level surface.

The normal reason for this defect is unequal settlement of principal wall posts and structural elements. Discussed earlier were defects resulting from a rotted principal corner post and the reaction this had on roof collars (see p101). Provided the floor construction itself is perfectly sound, such a defect gives a sense of age and character to the building as a whole. One could argue that unless a true and level floor surface is required for some specific purpose, there is no need to disturb the structure. This is probably a point to be settled by one's own personal taste; the writer left his floor with a noticeable lean which provided an enjoyable talking point.

There may be other contributory reasons for the defect, sometimes overloading the building to a point at which structural failure is likely. This commonly occurs when owners inflict very heavy furniture on a floor not designed or intended to bear such loadings. It also happens when an owner carries out alterations to the building to include the provision of extra partitions which may be fixed at a point in mid-span without the necessary propping or support from below. An owner may believe that a lightweight partition, constructed to divide a bedroom from a new shower-room, for instance, will not affect the overall performance or structural stability of the floor. In many cases he may be correct in his assumption, but the writer has surveyed many houses where such an addition has caused structural distress to the floor construction.

Another cause of floor sag is related to the removal of an intermediate support, perhaps because it obstructed the ideal place for a piece of furniture or did not fit into the interior design plan of the room. This often happens when a timber-framed house containing two small rooms at ground-floor level is altered to provide one large room. The original framing and floor joists may have been of too small a scantling to withstand the removal of an intermediate propping partition which, at first sight, might not appear to be structural. The removal of a partition for these reasons is also a very likely cause of excessive vibration in the upper-floor construction as a whole.

In the sections dealing with rot and insect attack (pp185–95), mention will be made of structural failure to wall posts and beams. Floor joists are also highly prone to attack from fungus and wood-boring insects. The ends of joists are a particularly common area of attack, especially if water has penetrated the outer wall claddings and soaked the timber structure.

In order to assess the cause of structural failure in floors, it is necessary to list the possible alternative reasons and carry out a logical process of elimination. If the failure is due simply to overloading, the loading should be removed at once. If, for example, a very heavy wardrobe were installed in a bedroom and the building showed obvious signs of distress, the item of furniture should be removed and placed elsewhere. This may seem obvious, but the writer can attest to many cases where the furniture has been allowed to remain and total failure of the structure has occurred. Many people believe that because a house has survived for a few centuries, it is indestructible. Nothing is further from the truth. A building survives simply because it has received a modicum of respect over the years, coupled with the fact that it is constructed with long-lasting and efficient natural materials.

Many period timber-framed houses now display exposed ceiling beams to ground- and upper-floor rooms; this allows relatively easy access to the woodwork and may provide a more ready answer to the defects. Assuming, however, that the ceilings are clad with lath and plaster or other ceiling finishes, it will be necessary to lift a few floorboards to check the joist sizes, spacing and connection details. The joist size is important when considering the overall span between walls or posts below. Modern buildings should be constructed in strict conformity to Building Regulations. The 1972 edition provides a table of modern joist sizes and recommended spans which are easy to refer to and compare. The period timber-framed house, however, is most unlikely to have a floor construction conforming with these parameters unless, of course, some exceptionally drastic course of action has dictated the complete removal of all original flooring timbers. In fifteen years of practice the writer has never experienced this.

Having lifted the floorboards, structural floor joists should be visible as, perhaps, will many years of dust and debris. You may also find signs of vermin and, if you are very lucky, coins, pins, buttons, jewellery and other personal artefacts small enough to have slipped down between the boards prior to the days of fitted carpets. If joist sizes and spans are suspect, an engineer should be instructed to provide calculations.

Medieval floor joists were usually somewhat over-designed, and large trees were cut or split to form joists which were commonly around 8 × 6in (20 × 15cm) in section. The writer's own house contained original oak floor joists of 8 × 7in (20 × 17.5cm) in part and 9 × 9in (22.5 × 22.5cm). These were set at very close centres giving an impression of immense strength (see Figs 75–7). Calculations for the loading capacity of this floor would require the services of a structural engineer.

When floorboards are lifted it may also be seen that the joists are laid flat, that is, with the largest dimension running across the top of the joist, whereas modern joists are designed with the maximum dimension on the vertical face. The reason for laying them horizontally is that a curved log could be halved over its length, thus avoiding a waste of timber (see Figs 75–7). The relatively straight edge or split face, which was usually the heart-wood face, was used as the surface to which the boards were fixed. Part of the character of an exposed-beam ceiling is the fact that the joists tend to bend and wander from side to side, thus creating an interesting effect. If the space between the joists is boarded, plastered and painted white, the overall effect is enhanced.

An inspection of floor joists should determine whether rot, insect attack, connection failure or something quite different is the cause of sagging or excessive vibration. The next stage is to explore further the ends of the joists and especially to consider bearing conditions at these points. Joists very commonly run from front to rear of a building, although they can also run across from gable to gable, or gable to party wall. In either case they are likely to bear upon an external wall at one end and a trimmer or bressummer at the other.

The decayed or structurally displaced end of a joist or joists will cause the floor to sag accordingly. Many timber-framed walls lean as a result of settlement over the centuries. It has been mentioned that the writer's house suffered from this defect at the gable end. If the

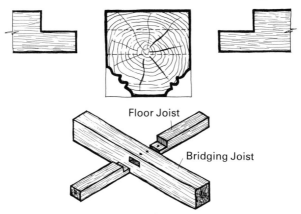

Fig 75 **Fourteenth-century bridging joist/floor joist detail.** Note the position of the joist tongue relative to the bridging beam.

155

Fourteenth–fifteenth century

Fourteenth century

Fifteenth–sixteenth century

Fifteenth–sixteenth century

Early sixteenth century

Sixteenth century

Late sixteenth century
deep chamfered

Seventeenth century
chamfered

Seventeenth century chamfered
with pyramid stop

Seventeenth–early
eighteenth century

Fig 76-77 **Ceiling beam details.** Various patterns dating from the fourteenth century to the eighteenth century.

wall leans outwards, the connection between the joist and the wall is almost certainly weakened. Movement in the wall would reduce the bearing surface of the joist end on the wall to a point at which it was no longer effective.

A common defect where this has occurred is wet-rot, which will further weaken the joist. If rot is local to the joist end only, the timber can be shortened by means of a new plate, a scarfing joint or a metal strap or hanger (see Fig 65). The exact method adopted will naturally

156

depend upon the extent of decay and the material and details of the wall.

If dry-rot occurs in the joist ends, all affected timber should be cut out and destroyed. Any masonry affected should be treated and the surrounding timber structure should be thoroughly inspected. A reputable timber infestation company should also be called in to examine the defects and to establish the cause.

Dry-rot is a very serious defect and can spread quickly to other parts of the building, causing damage likely to be very expensive to rectify. The cause of the dry-rot must be found and cured with all haste. A common cause is a leaking rain-water gutter or down-pipe and the consequent supply of water by ingress through the external walls and into the joist ends. There are many other causes, most of which could be avoided by regular maintenance of the building fabric.

By a logical process of elimination, it may be found that the floor sag is the result of movement around a partition. The partition may have settled over a number of years and subsequent cracks and small tell-tale signs hidden by years of internal cosmetic decorations. The problem may be overcome by means of a vertical post or system of posts and beams to the underside of the partition forming a prop. Very often the preferred remedy is a substantial beam spanning from one structural point to another, such as a wall to a wall, or a wall to a column. If it were thought absolutely necessary, then the upper floor might be jacked back into relative square before final insertion of the prop.

Never attempt this work without specialist advice, as damage to other parts of the frame could occur. The period timber-framed house is a complex of heavy structural posts, collars and trusses, many of which are held in tension and some of which are in compression. It may well be the case that certain essential structural members bear on upper partition walls. Any settlement of the lower structure would be reflected in the upper and side structures. The effect of jacking up a sagging floor could well cause tension joints to burst, with horrendous results to the remainder of the building. If a level floor is essential, the prop may best be inserted to avoid further movement and the floor levelled up by means of planted firring pieces. These are small fillets of timber cut to a taper equal to the degree of correction necessary.

A rolled steel joist of H-section is probably the simplest form of beam design. In this design three structural necessities are performed;

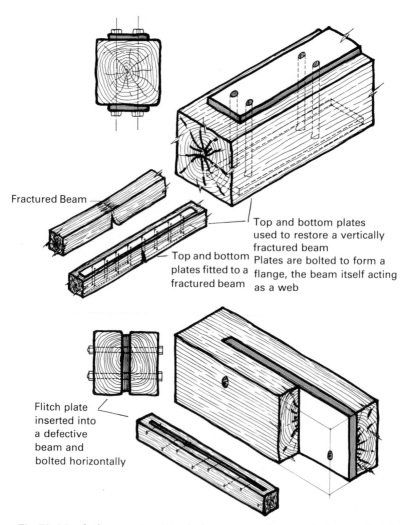

Fractured Beam

Top and bottom plates used to restore a vertically fractured beam

Top and bottom plates fitted to a fractured beam

Plates are bolted to form a flange, the beam itself acting as a web

Flitch plate inserted into a defective beam and bolted horizontally

Fig 78 **Metal plate repairs.** Metal plates are used to repair fractured timbers. See Figs 79, 80 and 81.

the upper flange is in compression, the lower flange is in tension and the web adjoining the flanges resists diagonal stresses between them while effectively holding them apart (see Fig 78). A medieval oak beam with joist mortices cut half-way up on either side is of very similar appearance to a rolled steel joist and performs a very similar structural role. A timber beam will always fracture on the underside first, demonstrating that the bottom edge is in tension and therefore the weakest.

Developing this simple mechanical theory, fractures to floor bridging beams and strengthening of floor members can be best repaired in one of the following ways.

Tension and compression plates A beam which has fractured on the underside can be drilled at regular centres and bolts passed through the holes to a compression plate laid on the top side of the beam, and a tension plate held on the bottom side. The plates should extend well beyond the line of fracture to give the repair adequate strength. The plates could be 3in (75mm) × ½in (12.5mm) although this will be determined by the size of the beam under repair and the prevailing circumstances. Once fitted, the bolts should be tightened and the plates drawn together. The writer has used this repair with excellent results and can attest to its value (see Fig 78).

The flitch plate This method of repair was used extensively in the last century. It comprises a metal plate set in a vertical position between two members which are later to be joined together. The flitch plate is, in effect, sandwiched between two timber beams and the three members firmly bolted together to form one member. Several bolts should be used and holes through the timber beams and flitch plate should be at variable heights so that the grain is not split when the bolts are tightened (see Fig 78).

The repair is strong because the flitch plate acts as the web of a steel joist but without the top and bottom flanges. The web is prevented from lateral movement by the provision of the timber members which give extra side support. This repair is probably best used on a bridging beam which is within a floor void for its entire length and joists framed into it on either side. The slot into which the flitch plate is situated can be sawn vertically for the full length of the beam while the side joists are left intact. The plate can be inserted into the slot and the bolts fixed and tightened without serious disruption to any ceiling finishes below. This method of repair has the approval of the Department of the Environment and is a common sight in restored buildings.

Bottom plate with upstand and steel wedges An overstressed beam will always fracture on the underside face first. Steel is perhaps the best material at resisting stress and this method of repair uses that principle. A flat steel plate is offered to the underside of a stressed timber beam and if the member is under permanent over-stress, can be strutted into position after the beam has been jacked up slightly.

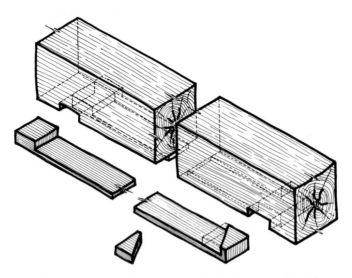

Fig 79 **Metal plate repairs.** An alternative method of repair and reinforcement of a beam. A bottom plate with upstand and wedges.

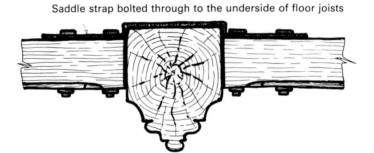

Fig 80 **Metal plate repairs.** A saddle strap repair to a moulded bridging beam.

In this instance, a welded upstand should be added to the ends of the plate and at one end the upstand shaped to a taper (see Fig 79). Once the beam is jacked up, the plate can be added and the upstands fitted to a recess in the underside of the beam provided. A steel wedge is then driven into the tapered upstand to grip the plate into firm position, at which time the beam and the plate become fully stressed. Strutting is then removed and the repair complete.

If the beam is not fully or permanently stressed, the plate can be offered up to the underside of the beam and bolted or coach screwed into place. This will work because the stresses are greatest in the centre of a beam span and, provided the plate is adequately fixed at each end, no other repair is necessary. If the fracture is in mid-span, the plate may not even have to extend to the ends of the beam for this reason.

SAGGING FLOOR JOISTS

Reference is made to two methods of support recommended by the Society for the Protection of Ancient Buildings. The first method uses a compression plate and tension cables. Here a plate is laid on the top face of the joists and the ends bedded into structural walls to either side of the room. The plate is coach screwed to the top of each joist to give a firm fixing. The ends of the compression plate are provided with a steel bracket bolted to the underside of the plate (see Fig 81). Holes are drilled through the joists at centres such that the central joists are drilled near the bottom edge. The position of the joist hole rises as the beam is nearer the outside wall (see Fig 81). When a tension cable is threaded through the holes it forms a curved section similar to that of a suspended bridge. Once the cable is stressed, the individual joists are lifted in centre span as though on a bridging beam. This method of repair may not be entirely suitable on medieval

Fig 81 **Strengthening of joists.** A repair using stressed cable and metal plates under compression.

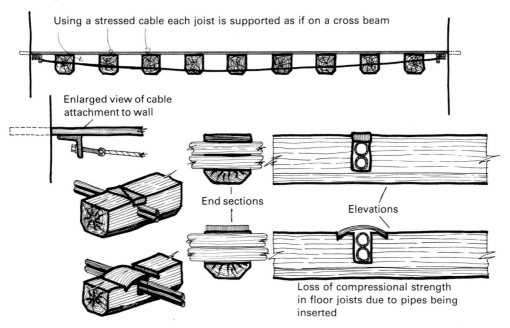

Using a stressed cable each joist is supported as if on a cross beam

Enlarged view of cable attachment to wall

End sections

Elevations

Loss of compressional strength in floor joists due to pipes being inserted

161

joists which are of substantial section, but the method is certainly worth noting.

Floors commonly sag because central heating or plumbing pipework passes through floor joists notched for the purpose. Even a substantial medieval joist has its limits and the writer has seen failure of a substantial member notched to provide free passage for three large bore-heating pipes placed one on top of the other. Notching of a joist can be safe if the cut is made close to a bearing point, ie near a wall or a supporting beam or post. The depth of the notch, however, should be watched carefully and if at all possible deep notches should be avoided. If the notch is near the centre of a joist span, a likely result is failure of the joist on the bottom or tension face. This can be rectified using two wedges hammered into position within the notch. This method assumes that the pipes are situated within the joist to an extent that a space is present above the top pipe and in which wedges can be placed. Should the top pipe be level with the top edge of the joist, as is often the case, notches can be cut to either side of the pipe notch. Metal plates formed with a slight curve in the centre should be laid so that their ends fit the notches provided and a bridge created above the pipe. The plates should then be screwed down as shown to either side of the pipe in order that compressional strength is returned to the top face of the joist.

ROTTED JOIST TENONS

The connection between a set of floor joists and a bridging beam is often found to be defective owing to rotting of the joist and tenons. Perhaps the simplest of repairs can be carried out using short iron plates screwed to the upper compression face of the bridging beam and the top face of the defective joists (see Fig 80). This repair is permanent in nature, simple to perform and often the floor structure need not be disturbed in the process.

ROTTED JOIST END BEARINGS

Floor joists commonly become defective at the end connecting to an external wall. In a framed building the external wall may be formed of the structural frame with infill panels of wattle and daub or brick. Water penetration through the infill panels might have rotted the bressummer upon which the joists bear. Alternatively, an area of brickwork or stonework constructed to first-floor level as an under-build to a jetty or replacement of the original ground-floor wall framing might be defective. It is likely to be extremely difficult to remove or replace floor joists in this position and it may not be practically or financially feasible to repair the decayed member with new oak. An alternative is the provision of a stirrup. This repair calls for removal of the rotted joist end until solid wood is located. If the beam were located in a wall pocket this should be properly filled in and made good. The stirrup may be fabricated from steel measuring 3in (75mm) × ¾in (19mm). It should be formed in two parts, the first part fitted to the underside of the joist and the second part set in and fixed to the top face of the joist. The space required between both stirrups should be about three times the depth of the joist. For example, if the joist measured 7in (175mm) × 7in (175mm), the space between the stirrups should be three times 7in, ie approximately 1ft 9in (525mm). The stirrups are held in position by metal bars measuring 3in (75mm) × ¾in (19mm), the projecting ends bearing onto a steel plate or padstone constructed in the wall. In a framed building, a steel plate properly treated with protective paint is the best alternative. The stirrups are not screwed or bolted to the joist and the end plate is not fixed in any way to the bressummer or wall.

Fig 82 **Repairs using timber.** A method of repairing the rotted upper face of a timber joist or beam. New timber is spliced in to replace the defective material.

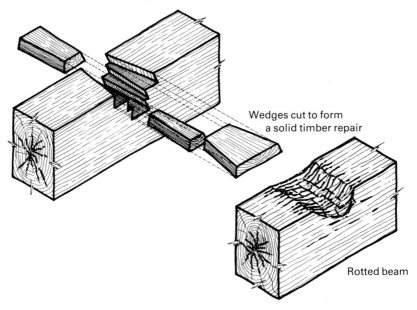

Wedges cut to form
a solid timber repair

Rotted beam

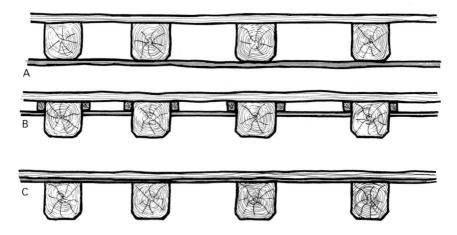

Fig 83 **Ceiling details.** Three methods of exposing or covering ceiling beams. The second method is probably the most adopted when beams are exposed. A) The ceiling is affixed to the underside of floor joists. Beams hidden. B) Floor joists are exposed and plasterboard strips nailed to timber noggins attached to the side of joists. A small cavity is formed. C) Joists are fully exposed. Ceiling board is fixed beneath upper floor boards and decorated.

The entire repair relies on gravity for its soundness. It is best adopted where the joist or beam is concealed within the overall thickness of a suspended floor.

Rotted bridging beams can be restored by splicing in new timber as shown in Fig 82 or by using plastic as discussed in the section on wall frames and shown in Fig 68. The rotted ends of a bridging beam can be repaired by cleaning off decayed wood, exposing sound timber and drilling 28mm diameter holes as shown in the figure. Polyester reinforcement bars of 28mm diameter are inserted into the holes and epoxy mortar poured in to fill any cavities. Epoxy resin forms an unbreakable adhesive connection between the reinforcement rods and sound timber. The method is fully discussed under wall frame repairs (pp116–22).

Each of the repair methods discussed shows ways in which joists or bridging beams can be made good with minimal damage or disturbance to the building. Unfortunately, poor repair, however well meant, often causes destruction and eventual replacement of principal members which might otherwise have been saved. Such drastic replacements cause a loss to the building as a whole and often valuable timbers are sacrificed as a result of negligence and plain ignorance on behalf of the owners or trustees.

4 THE FIREPLACE

Internal examination of a period timber-framed house, especially the roof space, may determine whether the building was originally an open-hall form. Positive confirmation of this may be made if smoke-blackened timbers exist, although sometimes dirt, grime and the ageing process can make identification of soot difficult.

The design of the roof may indicate whether the essential structure was intended to be seen. Some main beams, for instance, may be chamfered or moulded, or wind braces set in a decorative pattern to provide obvious ornamentation. If the roof was obviously intended for display but smoke-blackened timbers are not present, then it may be that a smoke bay or wall fireplace was provided or that the hall was a first-floor type.

Wrecclesham Farm House, near Farnham in Surrey, comprises two medieval hall house buildings with smoke-blackened rafters. The buildings abut at right angles and one is older than the other. The older structure of three bays has a clasped purlin and wind-braced roof which is completely blackened. An early sixteenth-century building was constructed at the west end at which time the old house became a kitchen. The newer building also had an open hall to which was added a smoke bay. Later, a brick chimney was built in the space occupied by the smoke bay and a great outside hearth added in the old building retained as a kitchen (see Plate 44). This example is especially interesting because of the double open-hall building. The same evolution occurred in other buildings throughout the country to provide the magnificent open or inglenook fireplaces loved and cherished by us today.

Chimneys constructed of brick or stone were unusual until the fifteenth century. In 1419 an ordinance of London ordered that no chimney should be built other than of stone, tile or brick. Wood and plaster were forbidden and it was threatened that a structure of these materials would be pulled down. The open hearth, however, continued until the end of the sixteenth century and brick chimneys were

Plate 44 **Chimney stacks.** The great stack at Wrecclesham Farm House near Farnham in Surrey. A loft is present at first-floor level. The building is a double open hall house and very unusual. It has been wonderfully restored and is now used as offices.

Plate 45 **Chimney stacks.** The gable end stack of a house in Hampshire. Note the lean and general shape of the structure.

often inserted into the open hearth as an improvement. In rural areas the smaller house had a hood constructed of heavy oak posts, beams and struts, with wattle-and-daub infill panels plastered on the inside against the heat. The wattle flue was daubed but not plastered. When the roof was thatched, as it often was in rural areas, the wattles extended through the thatch and formed a type of thatched chimney.

By the beginning of the seventeenth century, brick and stone were in common use and in 1662 Charles II introduced the Hearth Tax. Small cottages were excluded, but houses paid at a rate of 2/- for each hearth or fire and this added up to a substantial income for the country, reported as being around £200,000 per year. William III repealed the tax because of the hardship it put on many poorer people (see Plate 45).

On timber-framed houses the chimney stacks were built on an external wall because that position generally interfered less with the essential framing of the structure. During the sixteenth century it became common to build an 'axial stack' in the centre of the building – hence the name. The design started in the south-eastern counties and spread throughout the country. The success of the design encouraged owners to cut the structure of their houses and build axial stacks as an improvement. An advantage of the design was that the kitchen and parlour could be heated by a back-to-back configuration of the stack and even upstairs rooms could be heated.

Stone chimney stacks in Gloucestershire and the Cotswolds continued to be built on an outside wall, while in Devon, a stack on the front wall serving both floors was common.

During the eighteenth century, the axial stack gave way to the gable end stack (see Plate 45). This happened because the axial stack situated within the building took up too much room and provided a barrier to upstairs rooms. Moving of the stack structure allowed a third area to be incorporated in the centre of the house. This was usually unheated and became a hall and staircase space. The gable chimney stack also facilitated easier access to the bread oven which often projected beyond the building behind the fireplace.

Brick was generally considered the best material for the construction of chimney stacks. Its resistance to fire was better than stone and it was a more adaptable material. The large stacks of important houses were heavily decorated above roof level, but on a humbler cottage the shaft above the ridge was plain and square in section. On a thatched roof the brick shaft was designed with a projecting brick course above the point where the thatch abutted the shaft. This shed surface water from the joist ends where these connected to the brickwork. In other areas dressed stone was used and decorative features worked into it. The stone was not, however, as resistant to heat as brick.

STRUCTURAL CONSIDERATIONS

The structure of a chimney stack may be affected by two main factors. Broadly, these can be described as weathering erosion and settlement movement. Weathering erosion may affect the brickwork or stone structure or alternatively the bonding mortar.

Where erosion has affected brickwork or stonework, the entire chimney structure may be affected and weakened. If the erosion is not more than 25 per cent of the thickness of the chimney flue wall and the structure viewed in profile is reasonably plumb, it may be possible to leave the defect for the time being. If, however, the erosion is more than 25 per cent, individual bricks or stones should be cut out and replaced with others of a like kind and specification. The Society for the Protection of Ancient Buildings (SPAB) also suggest that due consideration should be given to 'plastic repair' as an alternative where appropriate.

Weathering erosion of mortar also causes a general weakening of the structure as a whole. Mortar erosion can lead to the characteristic lean of a period chimney stack into the direction of the prevailing rain-laden south-westerly winds. The weather side of a stack is more exposed to erosion and this leads to a gradual settlement of the structure accordingly. The effect is further exaggerated by slower drying out of the structure on the lee side causing expansion enhanced by the effects of frost attack.

Many old chimney stacks are now used as flues for gas- and oil-fired central-heating boilers. In a surprising number of cases, flue appliances are fitted without the provision of flue-liners. The result is that the products of combustion from either boiler type chemically attack the internal flue mortar, and acids are produced from condensing flue gases which in turn run down the internal brick or stone walls of the flue. Such action causes a weakening of the flue and is a contributing cause of uneven settlement in the structure and subsequent lean.

Remedial action is recommended by the SPAB and this can be summarised as follows:

> Rake out the joints to a depth of at least three quarters of an inch or twice the height of the joint, whichever is the greater. Re-point in a mortar mix of one part sand to one part lime to one part cement. Especial care should be taken to match the mortar colour and texture with that of existing pointing. It is best to keep the mortar back from the edge of the brick or stone to create a weathering drip. It is not recommended that the mortar be 'buttered' over the bricks. Coarser aggregate in the mortar can be exposed by lightly brushing over the area repointed with a soft brush before the pointing has had time to set.

If a chimney stack suffers from fracturing of brick- or stonework as a result of settlement owing to erosion or unequal loading, it may be possible to effect a repair quite simply by repointing. If settlement cracks break across whole stretcher bricks or complete stone faces, then it may be possible simply to remove these and replace with other bricks or stones of a similar type.

Settlement cracking may, however, be more extensive and the structure be in an overall poor condition. Viewed in profile, the stack may lean dramatically and mortar joints may also be extensively eroded. In such cases, the only real alternative is rebuilding. This is, however, a drastic step and one which may not occur very often. It is most likely that an owner will wish to keep the chimney stack in working order. The fireplace is, after all, a feature of any period house and the traditional inglenook opening one of the most important parts of any period timber-framed house.

A badly eroded chimney stack can be stabilised in situ provided that the cross-sectional dimensions are of sufficient size. Usually, the medieval inglenook will satisfy this requirement. The method used is as follows:

An asbestos-based pipe is lowered down the flue so that it falls in the centre of the opening. The pipe should be inserted so that a minimum space of 4in (100mm) is left between the outside face of the pipe and the inside face of the chimney flue structure. A concrete plug formed to a size sufficient to slide down the flue to a point where the flue bends or widens out is provided and this is held in place by means of ½in (13mm) reinforcing rods fixed at each corner of the flue opening internally. The rods should be long enough to reach the top of the flue where they are hooked and held in position by transverse rods resting on top of the chimney.

At the base of the flue a cut should be made in the structure to seal the gap between the flue and the inserted pipe. In effect, a ring is erected at the base of the flue at its connection with the pipe. As an alternative, and dependent upon the size and shape of the flue, it may be possible to cast around the base of the pipe a form of collar which will equally seal the pipe to the internal structure of the flue. Light steel grillage should then be lowered into the space between the internal flue and external face of the pipe.

The idea is to form a cavity between the internal 'lining' and internal face of the old flue. The grillage acts as a reinforcement. The space provided may be fairly limited and so a liquid mix of concrete will be necessary to pour into the cavity. Because of the necessary liquidity of concrete used, reinforcement is essential and should not under any circumstances be skimped upon. Once the concrete is set, the external face can be repaired as necessary by cutting out badly affected bricks and repointing.

It should be noted that if the flue is tall, it is best to carry out the work described in stages, pouring concrete in small quantities. It would be most beneficial to shore temporarily the external chimney structure with builders' boards and scaffold poles to avoid 'bursting' the flue during the process of concrete pouring.

In many cases, a chimney stack is only seriously defective in the upper reaches, being beyond the ridge line or external roof planes. In such cases, the top section of brick- or stonework may have split. Two main alternatives exist here: first, it may be best to demolish the upper defective section and rebuild in a manner closely matching the original. Secondly, the brick or stone joints can be raked out and wire ties inserted in each joint before repointing work (see Fig 85). It is important that the ties cannot rust as, after a relatively short while, the repair would become ineffective. Copper or stainless steel wire should be used to avoid this problem. Once inserted, the wire ties should be tightened and an equal strain imposed to avoid stressing the structure. The ties should be set against a firm mortar bed to avoid slicing the chimney, and repointing and cosmetic repairs then carried out.

If a chimney is especially tall and erosion has caused it to lean to a dangerous extent, then it is possible to jack the structure back to a vertical plane. To do this, the joints on the convex side of the lean should be raked out to form a 'hinge' around which the stack can be jacked. After jacking is complete, the concave side can be made good and any defective brick- or stonework replaced as necessary.

Where a chimney flue serves to exhaust fumes and gases from a gas- or oil-fired heating unit, an independent flue-liner should be installed. This is not just a recommendation but an absolute essential. Flue-liners commonly available are of the stainless steel type and these come in a variety of lengths and diameters. Such liners are designed for the purpose of converting a flue and can withstand the extremes of temperature inflicted on the structure with gas- or oil-fired heaters. Where a flue-liner has been installed it is essential that the top of the stack be sealed to avoid water ingress.

The inglenook fireplace chimney-breast is often capped at the top with a tall chimney-pot. This may be moulded or decorated and can look very attractive. Such a pot is unlikely to be an original feature and probably dates from after the seventeenth century. The purpose of the pot is likely to be an attempt at preventing down-draught with its associated problems. While the pot may look attractive, it may not be entirely stable and the SPAB recommend removal if this is the case. An alternative, but in the writer's view not such an attractive feature, is a stone slab laid over the flue outlet and raised up on four brick piers to a height of about 12in (300mm) (see Fig 84). This is a traditional remedy against down-draught and, to an extent, it stops surface rain-water and snow penetrating the flue opening. If it is

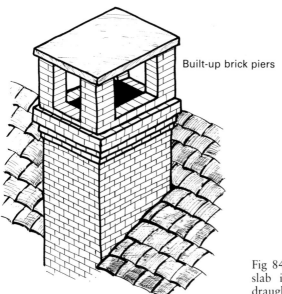

Built-up brick piers

Fig 84 **Chimney details.** A stone slab is used to prevent down-draught on an inglenook fireplace.

decided to maintain a decorative pot, whether totally in character or not, odd repairs may be needed before the pot can be rebedded. Such pots commonly fracture and become weakened. Repair is usually possible with sand and cement mortar and copper wire. Mortar, properly mixed, may be used to fill a fracture crack and can be disguised with a good brand of stone paint in a close matching colour. Copper wire can be used to bind the pot at top and bottom to ensure that it remains in one piece (see Fig 85). Stone paint will easily disguise the use of wire although, viewed from the ground, such a repair would be practically invisible even without paint. The SPAB recommend 'cannibalisation' of other damaged pots to effect a repair, but this is likely to prove very difficult in the majority of instances. Repair on economic grounds must be better than replacement. Genuine old pots are obtainable from antique shops and certain second-hand builders' merchants, but at a very high price. The writer has a collection of old pots gathered over a number of years. They provide excellent containers for trailing plants and stand proudly in a small courtyard near the house.

Chimney stacks are also a likely source of dampness ingress. Water may penetrate the flue owing to a lack of chimney capping. Many flues are left open at the top even though the fireplace which the flue serves is no longer used. The result is that rain-water penetrates the opening and birds nest in convenient holes provided. If the flue is

171

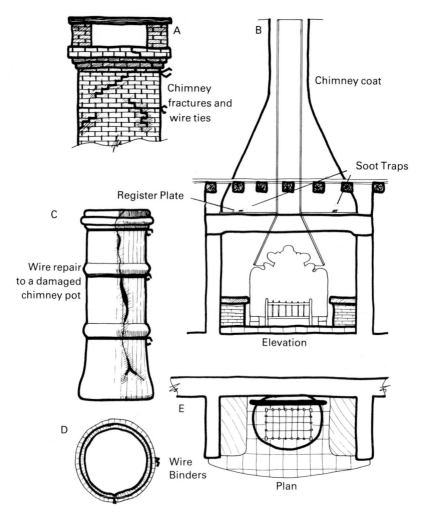

Fig 85 **Chimney details. Repairs to a stack and pots using wire ties.** 85B shows an internal flue to an inglenook fireplace to increase efficiency and improve draught.

capped, rain-water is prevented from entering and birds cannot nest, but the flue is also effectively blocked and any natural ventilation to the room in which the fireplace is situated is stopped. It is also true that a certain amount of water will penetrate a closed flue from sources other than the top opening. Any moisture entering the flue will not dry out very quickly owing to the structure being sealed.

It is probably best to maintain ventilation in a flue, especially in the type of flue most likely to be present in a period timber-framed house, and even more so if the chimney happens to be situated on an

172

external wall. Ventilation can be provided by bedding to the top of the flue a section of half-round ridge tile. This is laid the correct way up to form a type of bonnet or hat on the flue upper face. The ends should be left open to provide a flow of air while the tile shape sheds water away from the opening.

If the chimney stack is fitted with pots, which are an important feature in the overall appearance of the building, the following methods may be adopted to cap the structure. A piece of slate can be cut to match the size of the cross-sectional shape of the pot at the upper edge. The slate is then bedded onto the upper edge of the pot and the seal completed. This is a simpler exercise if the pot in question is square in section. Difficulty may be experienced in cutting slate to a perfectly circular shape. The second alternative may be best in this case. A sheet of lead is cut to the shape of the top edge of the pot but slightly larger to allow for dressing. The lead sheet is tucked and dressed over the lip of the pot to form a lid rather like the lid of a jam-jar. To provide ventilation, small holes can be cut in the lead and the material pushed up to form a small eyebrow over the hole to avoid moisture penetration. This is a relatively easy operation but requires some patience and a modicum of skill (see Fig 85).

Dampness can also enter a building via the flue at a point where it penetrates the roof. This problem is particularly acute when the flue is situated on an outside wall and adjacent to the roof eaves. The reason is the difficulty in providing a proper damp course between the two structures. Medieval houses tend to have steeply pitched roofs and this fact also compounds the problem. It is often difficult to provide proper and effective chimney flashings on a steeply pitched roof. The medieval chimney stack is unlikely to have a damp course unless it has been rebuilt. It therefore follows that unless the stack is in need of rebuilding, the lack of a proper damp course must be accepted. Chimney stack flashings should be regularly checked as a matter of course and renewed or repaired as necessary. Failure to do so will inevitably result in water entry to the face of the breast above the fireplace. If the fireplace opening is at ground level and a flue to a second fireplace exists at first-floor level, the dampness may manifest itself above this structure. Water penetration is bad enough, but the presence of salts and sooty deposits from the internal lining of the flue plays havoc with internal plasterwork and decorations. Once the plaster is soot stained it can be very difficult to conceal any damage cosmetically (see Fig 74, p150).

An alternative is to hack off the affected plaster and allow the breast to dry out. Subsequent replastering can then be carried out. If the problem is very serious, it may be worth considering battening out the wall using properly treated softwood battens. The process of tanalising wood is suitable in this context and 'tanalised' battens are readily obtainable at most builders' merchants. 'Newtonite' lathing may be used to cover the affected area or a vertical damp membrane formed using a bitumen paint such as RIW. Replastering can then be carried out over these alterations.

Water can also penetrate a chimney via the flaunching at the top of the structure. A simple repair can be effected by removal of the defective flaunching and new sand, lime and cement mortar applied. If the walls of a chimney stack constructed of brickwork are of inadequate thickness, water will simply penetrate and be a constant problem. A single skin of structure 4½in (112mm) thick will give this problem. Equally, water will freely penetrate the flue if mortar courses are eroded. It is essential, therefore, to check that brickwork is properly pointed at all times.

A disused chimney is likely to be damp to an extent even if ventilated. Hot flue gases go a long way towards drying out the interior of a flue and will reach areas which may not be easily ventilated. The medieval flue is commonly a straight open shaft of enormous size. It is impressive and a feature of many a timber-framed house. It is also a large opening to the sky through which water and snow can pour and soak interior structure right down to the hearth. The method of capping using a stone slab referred to earlier is therefore a good practical way to prevent water ingress of this type (see Fig 74, p150).

The effects of water penetration, together with those of age and use, can also affect internal 'withs' or brick dividers built into a flue to separate the main flue from secondary shafts. These frequently crumble or burn away, leaving a huge single opening to the sky.

In addition, the lintel carrying brickwork or stone structure may have smouldered away over the years, leaving in effect only a shell of the apparent scantling of timber on view from the living-room. It is unlikely that any pargeting to the flue remains and internal bricks may have crumbled and decayed with damage from soot, water and heat.

Where normal 'internal weathering' has taken place, it may not be necessary to do any more by way of redecoration than cosmetic improvement. Obviously, if the fireplace lintel is in an unsafe state it should be replaced. With some careful searching, it may not be too difficult to find a suitable length of old oak to use as a replacement.

174

One could argue that the lintel should be replaced with another of incombustible material which would almost certainly not be oak. It is possible to fix asbestolux strips to the rear or hidden face of a lintel to provide better retardant qualities to the wood. The danger is often not with exposed timber but that hidden away under masonry.

It is most likely that an inglenook fireplace, irrespective of condition, will be allowed to remain in a period timber-framed house and will become a feature and focal point of the room in which it is situated. The fireplace may only be used on special occasions as the house may have central heating. Much of the time it must provide an attractive setting for dried- or living-flower arrangements. It will be most embarrassing and annoying for the owner if on the day he requires the fire alight, the structure smokes. There are a number of likely causes of smoking fires and many can be solved relatively simply.

The purpose of a chimney is to dispose of smoke and any fumes from the hearth to the outside air. The chimney also draws in fresh air which helps to promote the fire. Common chimney faults can range from a nesting bird or inadequate draught, to highly technical problems requiring the attention of a chimney expert. Relatively simple causes of smoking can be local geography, ie the proximity of

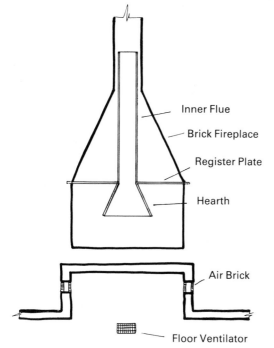

Inner Flue

Brick Fireplace

Register Plate

Hearth

Air Brick

Floor Ventilator

Fig 86 **Chimney details.** An inner flue with improved ventilation to gain extra draught without chimney smoking.

the chimney stack to high ground. Tall trees can cause problems, mainly associated with down-draught. The proximity of other buildings or even parts of the same building will cause problems if the formula is wrong.

Wind pressure and suction are common chimney-smoking problems. Modern Building Regulations stipulate certain standards to help overcome such problems, but the period timber-framed house was constructed at a time long before these regulations came into force. It is possible, however, to alter a chimney structure and perhaps create a better balance between necessary elements.

Building Regulations state that if a chimney is situated within 2ft (60cm) of the ridge or closer, it should project 2ft (60cm) above the ridge. Situated elsewhere on the roof and not close to the ridge, the chimney should be at least 3ft (1m) above the roof measured from the upper side. Where a chimney is situated within 2½yd (2.3m) of a dormer window top, it must rise at least 3ft (1m) above it.

There will be many instances where extra height is needed. Often an older house will have a chimney stack of the correct length due to trial and error over many years. Some houses will have very tall chimneys extending to well above the highest point of the roof ridge. Such a structure may help to avoid the problems of down-draught, wind pressure or suction.

As a rule, pressure builds up on the exposed side of the house facing into the dominant wind. An area known as the pressure zone exists on the weather side. If the chimney is situated on the weather side and within the pressure zone, the fireplace will probably puff smoke, and doors and windows rattle also. This is due to contesting pressures, drawn into the chimney from the roof and up it, and from ill-fitting doors and windows in the house.

On the leeward or sheltered side, opposite suction drags at the air supply and may actually reverse the flow of smoke in the chimney. A possible simple cure is to open a window or door on the weather or windward side and observe the result. This simple action may have the effect of letting air into the house, turning the building into a natural balanced flue. The period timber-framed house is likely to have air leaks through windows or under doors and this is necessary to feed an adequate supply of air to the fire. The fireplace may still smoke, however, so some other likely cause must be determined.

The most quoted authority on fireplace design is probably Count Rumford, an eighteenth-century American and chimney scientist. He stated certain principles of design which include the following:

176

a) The inside cross-sectional area of a flue should be one-tenth of the area of the fireplace front opening, and it should be square in cross-section.

b) The fireplace front opening should have an equal height and width.

c) The depth of the fireplace should be between one-third and one-half of the width of the front opening.

d) The sides of the fireplace should be splayed to reflect heat into the room.

e) The upper half or two-thirds of the fireback should be sloped outwards, also to reflect heat into the room.

f) Centrally above the fireplace should be a restricted throat 4in (100mm) from front to back, with its width determined by the splaying of the sides and back of the fireplace and the lintel over the fireplace opening.

g) Level with the restricted throat should be a smoke shelf. The purpose of the shelf is twofold: to prevent soot and rain from falling into the fireplace and more importantly to cause a two-way circulation of air in the flue.

h) Immediately above the restricted throat there should be a smoke chamber, the same depth as the flue, with sides tapering inwards at an angle of 60° until the flue is reached.

Count Rumford claimed that the amount of air needed to be introduced into the room to aid combustion was so small that no draughts would be caused as a result. The air needed to supply the flue would be provided by two-way circulation formed in the air currents.

These principles are fine but do not readily lend themselves to an early inglenook fireplace. They can be followed, however, in the alteration or insertion of a later fireplace, say, after the seventeenth century, the type of which is often found in period timber-framed buildings.

To stop an inglenook from smoking, other steps can be followed. The SPAB recommend methods found to work by many, including the author who has suffered from a choking inglenook! The first step is to place a stone cap over the chimney as previously described to help stop down-draught (see p170 and Fig 74). It is generally recommended that this is the best and most aesthetically desirable treatment for this problem.

As old buildings often have weak up-draught, this should be exaggerated where necessary. The typical inglenook opening is huge and the flues oversized. To cater for such openings a substantial flow of air is necessary or the fire will smoke. In its original form, the inglenook was used to burn oak or beech logs which, when properly seasoned and dried, might burn for days. The resultant heat build-up created a sufficient amount of hot air to remove smoke from the chimney.

Nowadays, however, we are told to save energy and our timber-framed houses may have fitted carpets or double-glazed windows. We have probably fixed draught strips around the doors and may have insulated the roof. These are all likely sources of air intake for a thirsty inglenook which will smoke without them. A simple test is to light the fire and wait until it smokes and then open a window or door to see the difference that the extra air flow makes. If the difference is substantial, then a general remedy is to increase the air supply to the chimney flue. There are a number of ways of doing this while still keeping doors and windows sealed. Briefly, these can be described as follows:

1 If the room in which the fireplace is situated has a timber suspended floor, remove a small section of carpet or covering and insert a 'hit and miss' grille immediately in front of the hearth. The effect may be surprising. To be properly ventilated, wherever possible a timber suspended floor should have ventilating grilles on all external walls. A flow of clean air is then able to enter the void to prevent a build-up of dampness which may cause rot. By installing a grille in front of the hearth, clean, fresh air is encouraged to enter the floor void and exit the building via the flue, thus creating a most effective flow. The writer installed such a system in a house which had the benefit of a cellar beneath the drawing-room. Air was encouraged to enter the cellar via ventilators provided for the purpose. A vitreous clay pipe was built into the suspended floor surface and bridged an area of solid structure at the base of the chimney stack below ground level. A 'hit and miss' ventilator gave an adjustable flow of air to the chimney flue and a variety of settings could be selected dependent upon outside wind strength and direction (see Fig 86).

2 The adjacent floor surface may be solid and it may be impractical to get a passage of air from an external wall to the flue via the floor. If an area of wall adjacent to the fireplace is externally mounted (see Fig 86), then it may be possible to place ventilators here to provide the necessary air flow. The writer has also tried this method, but in the example chosen was not very successful. It seemed

that whichever way the wind blew, the fire still smoked and eventually a chimney expert was sought.

3 An alternative with which the writer has had success is the installation of air-bricks or grilles to the return side walls of an externally mounted fireplace (see Fig 86). This alternative was cheap and easy to install and gave the most remarkable results. It is, however, important to remember that the combined unobstructed cross-sectional area of the inlets should not be less than the cross-sectional area of the flue.

The writer's house boasts an inglenook fireplace with an opening of about 7ft (2.1m) width, a height of 4½ft (1.3m) and a depth of about 2½ft (0.7m). The hearth is built up by about 4in (100mm) and a purpose-made hood provided with a drop of about 2ft (0.6m) below the oak fireplace lintel. We use an old cast-iron fire-basket rescued from a cottage many years ago. This is filled with coal and logs and stands about 9in (228mm) above the hearth. The space between the burning fire and the mouth of the hood is reduced considerably by this layout and we find that fires can be lit in virtually any wind condition without the fear of smoking (see Fig 85). We are well provided for draught, however, with ill-fitting doors and windows. Two rules apply here: the total volume of the flue should not be less than the total volume of the fireplace. The area of the fireplace opening should never exceed eight times the cross-sectional area of the flue.

We have also fitted an iron register plate at a point approximately 6in (150mm) above the underside of the oak lintel. This is at the soffit of the fireplace opening. Our steel hood is welded to the plate with an accuracy to be admired and a hole in the plate about 1ft 2in (350mm) formed. In any event, this hole should not be less than 1ft (300mm) in diameter. A long tube or liner is then welded to the other side of the register plate and this penetrates the brick flue (see Fig 85). To be effective, this tube or liner should be not less than 10ft (3m) in length. Our hood is circular in section and has a diameter of about 2½ft (0.76m). It could equally be square or rectangular in section, the design being a matter of choice. An ideal size could be an opening at the base of about 3ft (1m) × 2ft (0.6m) depth. The hood should generally be about 2½ft (0.76m) above the fire-bed, although this will vary with fireplace size and hearth design.

We are lucky enough to have an original cast-iron fireback to complete our inglenook fireplace. It is dated 1608 and came from a castle occupied by a family well recorded in history books. It was given to the author by the present head of the family and now has pride of position in his collection of artefacts. Firebacks which are usually decorated are intended to protect brickwork and structure at the rear of the fireplace from excessive heat and at the same time to reflect heat into the room. Properly set up, they can be most effective.

We have discussed structure of the fireplace and chimney stack and some recommendations have been given as to repair and restoration of defective flues. What, then, are the dangers of operating a fireplace in an unsafe condition? Obviously, the main danger is that of fire risk and in a timber-framed house this could be great. If the house has a thatched roof, then the danger is even greater and on no account should an owner light a fire until he is absolutely satisfied as to the condition of the chimney flue.

It is common in period timber-framed houses for ceiling bridging beams, floor joists or bressummers to be buried or partially contained in fireplace walls either on the surface or indeed inside the flue. The writer once entered the huge flue of a medieval inglenook to inspect internal cracking of the structure known to have occurred. Layers of soot and thick black cobwebs were lightly brushed away to reveal cracks in the flue brickwork and, believe it or not, a deeply moulded early medieval bridging beam which actually ran through the fireplace structure in one whole length without any account of the flue opening. It would appear that the fireplace was added, the position selected and brickwork built incorporating earlier first-floor structure, including a bridging beam. Floor joists originally connected the beam to an external bressummer beam. These had been cut and trimmers provided around the fireplace brickwork. Odd joists extended into the brickwork but were cut short of the flue opening. For centuries the inglenook had burned, but miraculously the bridging beam had only scorched on the bottom edge and sides. Damage was light and the mouldings clearly defined.

The risk which arises from hidden timbers in a flue, while great, is difficult to define. It is vitally important to ensure that a flue does not catch fire. This will occur if the flue is not swept regularly for it is not the brickwork which ignites but the soot deposited on it. A chimney fire can easily destroy a complete house at the worst, or crack a flue at best. The heat build-up in a burning flue can achieve 2,550–2,900°F (1,400°–1,600°C) and the noise can be terrifying.

How often an inglenook fireplace flue should be swept will depend upon the size of flue and regularity of use. Always consult a reputable local chimney sweep and seek his advice accordingly. Many chimney problems can be solved with a good clean. All too often people forget the job, or put it off to a later date because at the time it may not seem to be a priority. If an inglenook fireplace is fitted with a register plate, ensure that the plate is provided with at least two rodding holes through which the sweep can reach to clean above the plate. Two traps of, say, 9in (225mm) square should be provided, one to either side of the flue-liner or hood (see Fig 85). This is vitally important as the register plate is likely to be fitted in close proximity to the fireplace lintel. After a while, soot builds up around the internal liner and eventually drops off onto the upper face of the register plate. Were the plate not present, the soot would end up in the hearth. This occurs regularly after high wind, excessive rainfall or snow penetration. In time, the soot layer above the register plate becomes thick and solid in mass. It is both heavy and extremely dangerous. Heat build-up from a small chimney fire could ignite the register plate, build up and cause terrible damage. A very simple and practical method of sealing off access holes through the register plate is as follows: metal squares are cut from similar steel to that used in the manufacture of the register plate. If the holes are 9in (225mm) square, make the shuttering plates larger, say, 12in (300mm) square. This gives an overlap all around the hole of 1½in (38mm). The shutting plates can simply lay on the upper face of the register plate. In winter, place a brick over the shutting plate to increase its weight and hold it down in all conditions (see Fig 85). This design will be appreciated by chimney sweeps of both conventional and vacuum type alike who will find access to hidden parts of the flue considerably easier.

Chimney fires can also start as a result of alteration to the original flue layout. The original inglenook chimney stack is likely to have been a single open shaft to the sky. It is common, however, for later generations to add fireplaces in rooms adjoining the chimney stack. In the writer's own house, a Victorian flue was constructed in parallel to the original stack and at a suitable point turned through 90° into the original stack. At the point of turn, a soot box was installed to aid the chimney sweep in rodding out the flue. This had been neglected for many years and a build-up of soot in the bend created a serious fire risk. It is important, therefore, not to have several flues adjoining one chimney stack. It is equally important that bends in the flue are reduced to a minimum and that soot is not allowed to build up in them.

When climbing into the roof void of a period timber-framed house one enters a different world. Here, joinery has not been treated for cosmetic delight. Flaws in the structure can be clearly seen and spiders have a free range. It is always interesting to look at the chimney stack structure where it projects into the roof void and all too often it will have a tale to tell. It may have been noted from the outside that brick- or stonework has been repointed and flashings and fillets attended to. Internally, however, the brick joints may still be open and in need of repointing. The roof is likely to contain a good deal of dry, well-seasoned wood and this will ignite surprisingly easily from sparks escaping through open brick joints. It is essential, therefore, to ensure that internal flue brickwork is in sound condition. If the roof is thatched it may well be an idea to render the external flue brickwork in the roof void to be doubly sure of safety.

The flue of an inglenook is not likely to be pargeted or plastered internally. If, however, yours is, check the condition of the pargeting and make good where necessary. The effectiveness may be judged by carrying out smoke tests. Ignite a small smoke-bomb in the fireplace hearth and the coloured smoke will penetrate the flue. Any leaks will be readily seen either in surrounding rooms or in the roof void. A smoke-bomb can also be effective in establishing the cause of a smoking chimney as discussed earlier. If serious leaks are found it may be necessary to request that a specialist firm 'core' the flue. This process is more commonly known in drainage repairs and is very costly. Alternatively, an asbestos liner may be fitted, assuming, of course, that the flue is straight. This process has been discussed on p169. It is important to remember that stainless steel flue-liners are not suitable for use with normal open fires. This is because heat build-up in a flue is greater from an open fire and any soot catches on the internal corrugations of the liner, thus causing a substantial fire risk.

A common source of fire risk is the relationship between floor timbers and the fireplace hearth. At upper levels, in a bedroom for instance, the upper surface of the hearth may be level with the upper surface of floor joists. Often a building is refloored with new boards overlaying the old. At the hearth, new boards are cut around to form a hearth well. The edge of the boarding is then exposed to heat from the fire and ignition is easy. The hearth should always be at least several inches higher than the surrounding floor. Another fire hazard is the cracked hearth supported on timber framing to a suspended floor. This can occur at ground or upper levels and is potentially lethal. Many floor voids collect fluff, hair, wood shavings, scraps of paper and simple wood dust as a result of attack from common

182

woodworm. Ash from a hot fire spilling onto a cracked hearth can fall between the cracks and ignite the dust, causing a fire. The flame may not be immediate and the dust may smoulder for hours before finally bursting into life. The answer is to repair the crack and, if necessary, lay a new hearth over the old. As a general safety precaution it is always a good idea to keep a fire extinguisher near an open fire. Several placed around the house obviously reduce the risk of serious fire even more.

In this chapter we have looked at fireplaces and chimney stacks and discussed various methods of repair and restoration. The chimney stack is likely to be an essential part of the building and, as such, extremely valuable to its overall appearance. This does not mean, however, that all chimney stacks should be carefully preserved. Many older houses are added to and as a result new chimney stacks may be built. The writer removed an ugly Victorian stack which ran in parallel with an inglenook flue and created a fire hazard at an intersection in the roof void. The Victorian flue could have easily extended through the roof to form a separate stack. Had this been the case the writer would have removed the flue in its entirety and left only the original structure. There will, of course, be instances where removal of a stack is not possible or prudent. It is not therefore wrong to save the unwanted structure and make it safe as necessary. Equally, an original chimney stack may have become disused. Do not take it down, but rather leave it and make it weather-tight as a future owner may wish to reuse it. Only as an absolute last resort should a chimney in need of restoration be pulled down. Follow the methods of restoration discussed and make any repairs as inconspicuous as possible. Obviously, the choice between restoration techniques will depend upon the defect and how serious it is. Other factors to consider are accessibility, the position of the stack relative to other parts of the building and the consequences of leaving a repair until a later date. Each restoration job must be considered individually and common sense followed. The writer has had the pleasure of opening up a fireplace walled over in the 1950s and provided with a grey tiled surround of that period. Upon removal of the surround, plaster fell off the wall displaying an old lintel and iron straps supporting the structure above. The space which the fireplace occupied was vast and it was strongly expected that a substantial opening might be found beneath. Removal of a hidden Edwardian fireplace displayed the remains of a large Victorian opening. Beyond this, an earlier eighteenth-century opening became evident, as did a container load of rubble and soot. The original sixteenth-century opening was eventually discovered amid much excitement and speculation. As is often the case, the old oak fireplace lintel had been hacked to provide a better plaster key when the opening was reduced in size, but thankfully the beam had not been cut.

In another case, a complete inglenook in an intact state had been walled away during this century simply because the space it took up was no longer required. The fireplace, which had an opening of about 8ft (2.4m) in width, also had a spiral staircase running around it with the first tread to the right-hand side of the opening. At first-floor level, the room above had been increased in size and the hole in the floor through which the stairs ran had been filled in with new joists and boards to provide a level surface. Built-in cupboards were then placed over the old floor opening and fitted carpet laid. At first glance it was impossible to ascertain whether or not the building had a fireplace. Obviously, a check of room dimensions indicated that the space at ground-floor level was less than at first-floor level. The extra space at upper level had not occurred as a result of a split in the boundary, so a hidden structure was a likely reason.

The exposed fireplace was huge and its carved oak beam dated 1665 in the centre. Oddments of ironmongery were also walled away with it and, to the writer's knowledge, are in use today.

BREAD OVENS AND SMOKING CHAMBERS

When a bread oven was constructed it was usually near a fire with an opening direct to the fireplace. Many such ovens were added to an earlier fireplace in the eighteenth and early nineteenth centuries and this can be evidenced by changes in the structural brickwork. The ovens were usually brick-lined with an arched roof and sometimes fitted with a metal side-opening door. In Devon, ovens were commonly provided at the side or rear of a gable fireplace and protruded beyond the building. The oven was heated by filling it with sticks or brushwood which were set alight and the door closed. When the fire had burnt out, the ashes were raked clear and loaves placed inside. The loaves were placed in the oven using a long wooden paddle-shaped object known as a 'peel'.

Smoking chambers used to smoke bacon were mounted adjacent to the fireplace with an opening at low level and a flue above adjoining the main fireplace flue. The smoking chamber at Wrecclesham Farm House is an excellent example of such a structure (see plate 44).

5 WOOD-BORING INSECT AND FUNGAL ATTACK

By far the worst enemies of the period timber-framed house are rot and wood-boring insects. If allowed to develop uncorrected, they destroy the actual structural frame of the building and can, after a while, render the building irreparable in financial terms. Such buildings existed on a large scale only a few years ago and movement by sceptics and more importantly by the public health authorities and local authorities caused such buildings to be demolished and lost forever from our national heritage.

Various forms of rot can affect ground sills, the feet of principal and secondary posts, the upper surface of upper timbers in external wall panels and the end grains of bressummers and essential structural timbers bearing on external walls. Rot is common in structural joints and can cause a building literally to burst as some timbers are under constant tension. The feet of braces in external walls are very prone to the problem, as are the lower ends of studs and joints between beams with posts. Window-sills are a common entry point for surface water, especially near the sill ends or horns. If the building has walls constructed of brick panels set into the timber frame, water will in time freely penetrate the space between the mortar, masonry and frame. It does not matter how carefully a restorer points the panel of brickwork where it abuts the frame as movement – albeit very slight – will be enough to allow the ingress of surface water into the frame and thus into the building. For this reason, mastic jointing is an absolute necessity.

Because wood is an organic material it is subject to two main categories of decay: first, fungal roots which attack the structure of the wood and break it down into a hopeless and pitiful form; second, the effects of wood-boring larvae.

Any well-ventilated woodwork will not suffer from any of the normal forms of fungoid disease as they require a high humidity before they can germinate. Wood-boring beetles thrive on a combi-

185

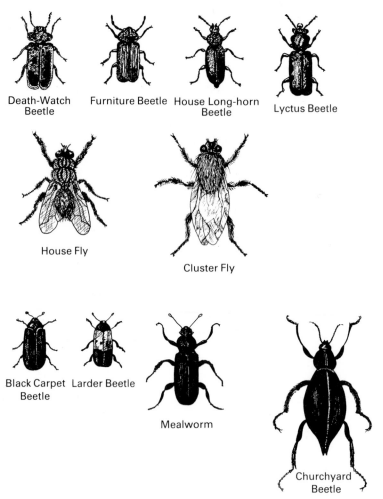

Fig 87 **Common house pests.** The most common insect pests to be found in a period timber-framed house.

nation of warmth and darkness; many timber-framed houses provide an ideal breeding ground for these unwelcome visitors. The problem is all too often compounded by insulation of the main roof whereby the essential timbers are covered on the outside and a heating system is provided on the inside. Trapped heat maintained throughout the year provides an ideal climate for the common furniture beetle (*Anobium punctatum*) and the death-watch beetle (*Xestobium rufovillosum*). The furniture beetle, which achieves a length of $1/10$–$1/5$in (0.25–5mm), will attack any softwood and is the commonest wood-boring insect in this country. It can be found in virtually any timber used in construction and is perhaps most prevalent in roof areas and floor voids. It also has a habit of eating furniture, usually from the underside, where it is able to feed unnoticed. The death-watch beetle achieves a length of ¼–⅓in (6.25–8.3mm) and thrives on oak, although it will also attack other hardwood. It is generally prevalent on old seasoned timbers and prefers them to be of substantial section. Like the furniture beetle, the death-watch beetle will also happily eat furniture but its flight holes are on a somewhat larger scale.

The powder post beetle (*Lyctus*) will eat the sapwood of a hardwood member, turning the structure to powder. It generally prefers well-seasoned wood and achieves an overall length of about ⅕in (5mm). The house long-horn beetle (*Hylotrupes bajulus*), achieving a length of ½–¾in (12.5–18mm), is the last main group of pest beetle. It is perhaps the most destructive of the beetle pests and has become prevalent over the last twenty-five years. Essentially, it attacks softwood and is difficult to detect as it rarely leaves flight holes or gives any indication of its presence.

When carrying out a survey of a period timber-framed house it is essential that a reputable timber infestation surveyor be instructed to survey all exposed timbers and to report in the fullest terms on his findings. The presence of the common furniture beetle in almost any house is taken for granted these days. The death-watch beetle is less expected, but still common in timber-framed buildings. The powder post beetle can produce a shock to the surveyor when he grasps an apparently solid member for support in a dark and dusty roof void and suddenly it falls apart in his hands. The writer remembers the result of a death-watch beetle attack on a substantial principal rafter which, when stressed, literally fell to pieces. Such examples can cause an owner considerable expense and annoyance. Always have a thorough survey before you buy a house, not just before you decide to restore it.

To compound the problem, the co-existence of fungal decay and beetle infestation is extremely common. The reason for this is that by nature the old hand-made clay-tiled roof is likely to be laid on battens which in turn are nailed to the outside edge of the rafters. On a modern roof, Building Regulations require the inclusion of a waterproof sarking felt to be laid between the tile battens and the rafters. The felt stops surface water from gaining access to the roof void and damaging structural timbers. It is possible when reroofing an old oak roof to include sarking felt in the specification, but in the opinion of the writer such a detail should be avoided as the felt prevents the natural flow of air entering the roof void from under the tiles which can cause all sorts of nasty problems in a roof that is either not easily accessible or not used on a regular basis. Alternatively, the roof void should be well ventilated by other means. The lack of felt on an old roof can, however, allow rain-water or snow to enter the void and create conditions of local humidity for perhaps just long enough to encourage an outbreak of dry-rot or wet-rot. Unless by chance the outbreaks were discovered soon and treated immediately, a local infestation is likely to spread rapidly throughout the roof and cause considerable structural damage to affected timbers.

It so happens that these conditions are also favourable to three main species of beetle which have been mentioned. Some forms of wood-boring insects attack wood only when a fungal attack has taken place. In biological terms, the exact role of the fungal attack is not thoroughly understood, but the existence of a relationship is certain. For the death-watch beetle to flourish, fungal attack is a pre-requisite. It has been suggested that the beetle previously attacked standing oak which was then utilised in the construction of buildings. Several types of fungi are likely to have caused infestation of the wood in its standing form, including the commonly known cellar fungus (*Coniophora cerebella*). Large infested timbers were likely to have been sited in areas where dampness and poor ventilation were problems, and in these cases the fungal decay was kept alive and perhaps even intensified. The death-watch beetle is also closely associated with *Merolius lacrymans*, the dry-rot fungus, although the beetle attack is more common on soft- rather than hardwoods when the fungus is present. It is important to remember, however, that oak attacked by the death-watch beetle has not necessarily decayed to a point at which a substantial loss of strength occurs. For example, difficulty can be suffered when trying to saw through a member which has a death-watch beetle attack in association with the fungus *Fistulina hepatica*, which gives the wood the name 'brown oak'.

The wood-boring weevil belonging to the *Curculionidae* family is generally found around the country, but used to be most common in eastern counties. The weevil is found infesting badly ventilated and damp wood, especially where a wet-rot fungus is present. The weevil will attack both soft- and hardwood and is often found around hard-wood timbers laid against a structure without any form of damp course: joist ends and wall plates adjoining masonry are likely points of attack. In one instance, part of the lower framing of a timber-framed house had been replaced by 9in (22.5cm) brickwork, the work of a well-meaning Victorian builder. The brick structure was not provided with a damp course and was consequently extremely wet. The weevil had lived happily in the ends of the first-floor joists where these rested on damp masonry and had also attacked horizontal first-floor beams in the immediate vicinity. The typical weevil is cylindrical in appearance and about 1/12–1/6in (2.4–4mm) in length. The larvae are white and legless, and flight holes formed when the creature eats its way out of the wood are circular with ragged edges.

The fourth type of beetle which lives on timber affected by fungal decay is the wharf-borer (*Nacerdes melanura*) which is a very large insect achieving an overall length of 1/4–1/2in (7–12mm). It is frequently confused with the common soldier beetle which is a relatively harmless insect found in the countryside. It was known to infest wharf timbers, largely hardwood, which became saturated from time to time as water levels varied and where fungal attack was taking place. To survive, the wood should not be much above fibre saturation point as the larvae of the beetle are prone to drowning. The beetle is a particular pest in timber-framed buildings and especially where a structure is kept damp below ground level. In this instance, lower ends of posts, and especially ground sill beams, are all liable to attack.

Generally, all of the wood-boring insects which attack timber partially decayed by fungi have the effect of accelerating the destruction of the timber to such an extent that it can no longer perform its function. The structural timbers in a period timber-framed house rely on strength around joints for rigidity. If this function is threatened by a weakening of the structural members concerned, serious problems will occur.

FUNGAL ATTACK

Generally speaking, the fungi which attack timber in any building can be divided into two categories: wet-rot and dry-rot. They only ever attack wood that is wet, but dry-rot is able to carry its own moisture to otherwise dry wood and thus spread the infection. Wet-rot is unable to do this and is generally confined to areas kept damp by, for instance, rising dampness, penetrating dampness or even a leaking pipe or tap.

As temperature rises, the fungi in both categories become more active and problems often occur in buildings after a central heating system has been installed. The old-fashioned paraffin heater and the popular portable gas heater are also friends of the fungi as they give off water vapour which is their life-blood. Some fungi live off the cellulose contained in wood but do not attack the dark lignin. Others also extract the lignin, reducing the wood to a white fibrous material – hence the names white-rot and brown-rot.

The wet-rot family includes the cellar fungus (*Coniophora cerebella*), the oak fungus (*Phellinus megaloporus*) and the pore fungus (*Poria vaillantii*). The cellar fungus, despite its name, does not only attack in cellars but can be found wherever damp wood is situated. It is possible for the fungus to be actually inside the wood and not clearly visible on the surface, but, when visible, it takes the form of a very thin brown and yellow skin, sometimes with brown strands. Cellar fungus can be categorised as a brown-rot and will attack both hard- and softwoods, turning them an exaggerated shade of dark brown.

Restorers are sometimes confused by oak fungus as it does resemble dry-rot. When the two are closely compared, however, it will be seen that oak fungus is hard and can be difficult to break away from the wood, whereas dry-rot is soft and easy to part. Oak fungus weeps in a similar manner to dry-rot, but the droplets of water are of a brown or yellow colour, unlike the clear drops of dry-rot.

Pore fungus appears on the wood as an opaque sheet and grows strands of similar description. It is common in buildings where the timber frame has been exposed to damp, such as a leaking gutter around a wall plate or post. Pore fungus needs a higher moisture content in wood than the dry-rot fungus to thrive, and it will continue to flourish up to a temperature of 97°F (36°C) which would halt the growth of dry-rot. Only softwoods are affected by the pore fungus, but it can spread to continuously wet hardwood. The decayed timber is generally darker in colour than the unharmed. It will not spread to dry timber beyond the area of wetness from whence it began.

Wet-rot fungi will attack timber in any location provided the conditions are suitable. The undersides of ground-floor suspended floors are a very common point of attack, as are small and restricted roof voids with poor accessibility, such as those under a low-pitch or

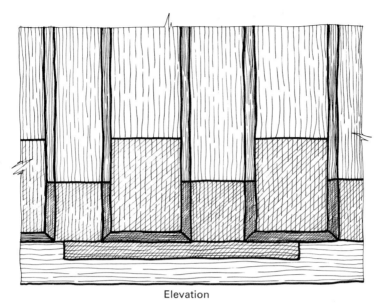

Elevation

New timber spliced in

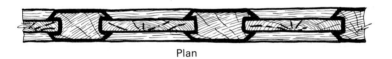

Plan

Fig 88 **Internal wall panel repairs.** This method shows new timber spliced in to replace old decayed wood.

flat-roof area. The writer has found fungal attack in the voids of ceilings where the ceiling panels have been fixed directly to the underside of sloping common rafters in order to achieve a reasonable height in a roof space. The void has been poorly ventilated, resulting in constant dampness from the elements. It is most important always to leave adequate ventilation in the roof space, hence the author's objection to the use of sarking felt, particularly in an oak roof. Unventilated oak is prone to a high amount of sweating.

Wet-rot is very common in the subfloor voids of ground-floor rooms, particularly where inside timber suspended floors are situated with their upper faces below outside ground level. This effectively means that the subfloor void is a sump below ground level into which water will collect and remain. The medieval timber-framed house has

Plate 46 **Wood decay.** An example of wet rot attack to an external window on a north facing wall (Hampshire).

a complicated structure of posts bearing on sill beams, all of which are likely to be at, or below, ground-floor level. In many instances where the structure is below ground, fungal problems can occur in the main structural frames, even when sills are above ground level and the subfloor void is adequately ventilated by means of air-bricks and grilles.

Very often an owner will decide to have a flower-bed immediately adjacent to the external walls of the house, causing air-bricks or grilles to become blocked by soil levels banked up against the lower walls of the house. Alternatively, wet and bushy plants, grown immediately in front of grilles, drastically limit the flow of air to floor voids. In one instance, an elderly lady planted miniature rockery plants in the ventilation grilles because she thought the walls could do with some brightening up! It follows, then, that whenever a subfloor void is present at ground-floor level, ventilation of the void is vital to prevent fungal attack to the substructural timbers. It is always a good idea to cut a small hatch in a timber suspended floor through which a regular inspection can be made of the void. Often the void is very shallow, but the provision of some limited entry avoids the inconvenience of removing whole floorboards when an inspection is necessary. Always keep external wall ventilators free of soil, plants, dried leaves and rubbish as this simple point can save a tremendous amount of expense, upheaval and heartache.

DRY-ROT

The dry-rot fungi (*Merulius lacrymans*) is so named because it leaves wood it has attacked in a dry, friable and shrunken state of condi-

192

tion. Similar to *Phellinus megaloporus*, *Merulius lacrymans* is not a forest fungus but is peculiar to buildings. It thrives in neglected or poorly maintained areas. When present in large quantities, the spores are a rusty-red or mustard-yellow colour. They accumulate in unventilated conditions where dampness is present. Sometimes it is possible to see the spores captivated in a spider's web when some breeze has blown them from the sporophore. The mycelium external to the timber is in the form of thin silvery-grey sheets tinged with patches of lilac colour or bright yellow. When in damp conditions, the mycelium grows rapidly and becomes snowy white, taking on the appearance of cotton wool. Where there is dry material or exposure to light, the colour changes to bright yellow. The name *lacrymans*, which means weeping, refers to the globules of water which form on the fungus in damp conditions when in active growth. The generic name *Merulius* refers to the yellow colouration on the mycelium and is derived from the word *merula* being the colour of the beak of a male blackbird. Wood attacked by dry-rot contains deep longitudinal and transverse fissures which cause the material to break up into cubes which can be up to several inches in length. The cracking described is seen on the surface of the wood.

Because the fungus has extracted cellulose, the wood becomes light in weight, dark in colour (usually very brown), is ultra friable and loses its fresh smell caused by the resin contained in it. The fungus is able to produce water-carrying strands called 'rhizomorphs', which are formed from hyphae into vein-like structures which may be the thickness of a lead pencil. The purpose of the rhizomorphs is to carry water from the already decayed damp wood to drier wood and so spread the infection. The fungus is not only active on wood but is able to convey itself over metal, stone and brickwork. The rhizomorphs are able to travel considerable distances and are capable of penetrating brickwork and of boring through mortar joints, thus spreading decay to other parts of the building or even adjoining buildings through party walls. If the atmosphere is moist and still, this can happen in weeks rather than months. Much of the infected wood is liable to be in a position where it is difficult to detect, so smell becomes an important clue to detection. The smell of dry-rot is highly characteristic and has been likened to the aroma of toadstools or rotting mushrooms, although this tends to be a matter of opinion. First signs that dry-rot fungus is at work are strange smells and the falling from ceilings or wall cracks of reddish-brown dust which is the airborne spore of the fungus. As stated earlier, the dry-rot fungus can be confused with the wet-rot fungus (*Phellinus megaloporus*), but the main difference to remember is that the sporophore of the dry-rot fungus, which in later life takes the appearance of a pancake, is leathery to touch whereas the *Phellinus megaloporus* is hard.

Merulius lacrymans is not as common as *Coniophora cerebella*, but is of far greater danger to the structure of buildings. Once a building is affected, it is most important to rid the structure of every trace of the fungus as failure to do so will only cause a reoccurrence of the infestation.

ERADICATING WOOD-BORING INSECTS
AND FUNGAL ATTACK

Eradication advice for these two destroyers is simple: consult an expert. Do-it-yourself campaigns are satisfactory if the pest damage is light and access to the timber is straightforward. It is, however, vitally important to remember that modern insecticides are strong poisons and while they may be effective in killing insects, they may also be effective in harming humans. They should never be used in tight, enclosed areas without adequate ventilation as the fumes they give off can be extremely harmful.

Insects most commonly found in timber-framed houses are the common furniture beetle and the death-watch beetle. Damage from the furniture beetle is most likely to affect sapwood only of an oak frame, unless the wood has become wet over a long period of time. The furniture beetle is more likely to eat furniture and softwood where the going is easier.

The death-watch beetle produces a much larger flight hole than the furniture beetle and will attack both oak and softwood. Damage to oak, especially the inner heartwood, is likely to be moderate unless the wood has been exposed to extreme dampness. One of the most likely places to spot damage by the death-watch beetle is around surface water guttering which has leaked over a period of time soaking surrounding structure. Often an attack will not be obvious until it is too late and substantial restoration expense may be necessary.

Both species of beetle have a long life span, spending up to five years as larvae before finally emerging as adult beetles. This life cycle can be speeded up in an ideal environment, and damp, unventilated conditions produce such an environment. Emergence of the beetle happens in about April through until June of every year when piles of

194

dust on the floor indicate movement. The death-watch beetle also ticks at this time, its sound being the characteristic mating call so well known to owners of old houses.

Treatment of insect attack should be left to the experts as identification of the beetle is not always straightforward and action not always entirely simple. Oak beams can lose much of their bulk before becoming unsound structurally and a good wood preservation surveyor will recommend that surface flack wood of a member be removed prior to treatment by chemical spray. This action will avoid chemical fluid being soaked up in waste wood and will enable the preservative to penetrate structural timber.

Eradication of fungal attack is on similar lines and again the expert's advice should be sought. Assuming fungal attack is of the wet-rot family, the first task must be to cut off the supply of water to the fungus. Any necessary building repairs should be carried out to perform this task before treatment of infected woodwork. Once the wood starts to dry out, the fungus will die and it may be necessary to replace only the parts of a timber member most affected by the fungus. A rotted joist, for instance, can be repaired along the lines of repairs discussed in the section on suspended timber floors (see Figs 68 and 82).

If, however, fungus attack is from the dry rot family, the task is more serious and difficult. Such a fungus requires moist timber for germination, but once this is satisfied it can travel over and infect dry timber, taking its own supply of moisture with it. Drastic measures are needed and often these entail removal of large portions of timber well beyond the last area of attack to ensure that no trace of fungus is left remaining. Any structure in proximity of the affected wood should be heat or chemical treated to destroy all spores, and woodwork within about 1yd (1m) of the last point of attack should be removed and destroyed, preferably by burning. It is, therefore, important to establish which of the rot families an outbreak belongs to.

A period timber-framed building is likely to contain at least some moulded timbers worth preserving at all costs. It would be terrible to remove a timber suffering from rot in the belief that it was dry-rot when in fact it was wet-rot and simple eradication of the dampness and local repair of the member would have sufficed. This must have happened over the years and valuable timbers lost accordingly.

Yellow Pages is a good source of supply for names and addresses of timber preservation companies.

APPENDICES

1 ORGANISATIONS AND AUTHORITIES CONNECTED WITH HISTORIC HOUSES

DEPARTMENT OF THE ENVIRONMENT, 25 Savile Row, London W1X 2BT

ROYAL COMMISSION ON HISTORICAL MONUMENTS, Fortress House, 23 Savile Row, London W1X 2HE

HISTORIC BUILDINGS BUREAU, 25 Savile Row, London W1X 2BT

HISTORIC BUILDINGS COUNCILS FOR ENGLAND, SCOTLAND AND WALES, 25 Savile Row, London W1X 2BT; *or* 25 Drumsheugh Gardens, Edinburgh EH3 7RN; *or* 22nd Floor, Pearl Assurance House, Greyfriars Road, Cardiff CF1 3RT

NATIONAL MONUMENTS RECORDS FOR ENGLAND, SCOTLAND AND WALES, Fortress House, 23 Savile Row, London W1X 2HE; *or* 52–4 Melville Street, Edinburgh EH3 7HF; *or* Edlestone House, Queens Road, Aberystwyth, Dyfed, Wales

SOCIETY FOR THE PROTECTION OF ANCIENT BUILDINGS, 55 Great Ormond Street, London WC1N 3JA

ARCHITECTURAL HERITAGE FUND, 17 Carlton House Terrace, London SW1Y 5AW

ANCIENT MONUMENTS SOCIETY, St Andrew by the Wardrobe, Queen Victoria Street, London EC4

VERNACULAR ARCHITECTURE GROUP, Chyan Whyloryon, Wismore, Leominster, Herefordshire HR6 9UD

HISTORIC HOUSES' ASSOCIATION, 10 Charles II Street, London SW1

GENERAL
Local authority planning offices, local museum and local amenity societies all offer help and advice to owners of old houses. Lists of Buildings of Special Architectural or Historic Interest can be inspected by anyone at the local planning office at either district or county level.

2 SPECIFICATION FOR THE REPAIR OF DAUB IN WATTLE-AND-DAUB WALLS

Specifications for the repair of daub vary, as much depends upon local materials and traditions. It is, however, possible to offer a general specification, which should be mixed as dry as possible to reduce shrinkage, and limewashed afterwards to protect against the elements.

Mix 4 parts of white lime putty with 1 part of sharp sand and with 1 part of cow dung (the cow dung is best in slurry form).

The above components should be well mixed with 6in (150mm) chopped straw or hair to act as a binder. When beaten together, the mix should be applied in one good coat to both sides of a wattle which has already been suitably repaired, or to a lath or mesh panel if these are substituted. The mix should be allowed to dry, whereupon shrinkage cracks should be filled with a similar mix, excluding the straw or hair binder. The best finish can be obtained by using a wood float.

GLOSSARY OF TERMS

ADZE A medieval carpenter's tool used to shape oak members.

AISLED HALL A hall divided into two or three aisles with lines of posts and arches lending support to the roof structure.

ARCHITRAVE A piece of moulded timber covering the joint between a wall face and a door- or window-frame.

ASHLAR Timber studding, often plastered, used to cut off the angle between the roof line and the floor. Also the name given to stone blocks cut into smooth and rectangular shape laid in regular courses and with very fine joints.

BALUSTER The vertical member supporting a hand-rail on a staircase.

BARGEBOARD Often referred to as a verge-board. A piece of board fixed to the verge of a roof. On timber-framed houses, the barge- or vergeboard covers the otherwise exposed ends of both wall plates and purlins. This detail, which originated in timber-framed houses, was later common on stone and brick buildings for the same purpose.

BASE CRUCK A cruck frame of truncated section which stops short of the roof ridge.

BATTEN A thin strip of wood used in roofing. Usually less than 1 × 2in (25 × 51mm) in size.

BAY The definition of a space between two principal roof trusses or between a truss and an end wall.

BOND The name given to the pattern of laying bricks in a wall.

BONNET TILES Shaped tiles used to waterproof the hip of a tiled roof.

BOX FRAME The name given to timber-frame construction in which the walls support the roof and upper-floor construction. All members are framed together to create a box-like structure.

BRACE A diagonal member in a frame used to strengthen the structure.

BRACING-PIECE A timber member framed diagonally into two other members each framed to form an angle. The bracing-piece forms a triangle between the other members and may be in tension or compression.

BRACING-STRUT A bracing piece but held in compression.

BRESSUMMER In period timber frames, the upper sill spanning an opening and supporting a wall above. Could also be the sill of the upper wall above a jetty.

BRIDGING BEAM A large floor beam often chamfered or moulded, used to support the ends of common floor joists.

BUILDING REGULATIONS A set of statutory regulations detailing standards of construction in building. These should be observed when altering or extending a period timber-framed house, although in certain circumstances exemptions may be given.

BUTT PURLINS An alternative name for tenoned purlins. These are jointed into the principal truss with a tenon joint.

BUTTERY Part of the service area used for the storage of drink.

BYRE An attached or separate building intended to house animals. In long-house construction it is commonly the lower end.

CAMBERED BEAM An angled beam, often curved, the central portion being higher than the ends. Cambered beams are often used as collar or tie-beams and are commonly thought of as being ships' timbers.

CAME The name given to thin strips of lead used to retain the 'quarries' or panes of a leaded-light window.

CAP OR CAPITAL On a crown-post roof, the upper part of a shaft usually moulded and designed to receive an arched superstructure.

CASEMENT WINDOW A window hinged at the side.

CATS Straw and clay rolls used to infill between the timbers of a period-framed building.

CAT-SLIDE ROOF A roof constructed with the main slope extending uninterruptedly over an extension. In Hampshire often referred to as a 'Hampshire roof'.

CELLAR FUNGUS (*Coniophora cerebella*)

Common wet-rot fungus.

CHAMFER The removal of the underside corners of a beam for decorative purposes.

CHASE A groove cut into a member to receive the edges of panelling or framing on a plastered wall.

CLADDING Can be of tile, boarding, lath and plaster, etc, used to provide an outer skin to walls.

COLLAR The horizontal member joining a pair of rafters and creating triangulation in the structure. Usually situated above plate level.

COLLAR BEAM A horizontal timber situated above wall-plate level spanning between and tying together a pair of rafters.

COLLAR PURLIN OR CROWN PLATE A horizontal member running longitudinally in a roof under the centre of the collars. Found in crown-post roofs.

COMBED WHEAT REED A thatching material which is in fact straw and not reed.

COMMON FURNITURE BEETLE (*Anobium punctatum*) A common wood-boring insect which attacks timber in buildings and furniture.

COUNTER BATTEN To lay battens beneath or above other battens but at right angles to them.

COWL A fitting to a chimney designed to increase up-draught.

CROSS-WING A two-storied transverse section comprising a large open-halled apartment and landing at first-floor level. Service rooms were probably contained at ground-level below.

CROSS PASSAGE A through-passage running across an open hall and separating it from the service areas.

CROWN POST A vertical post, often decorated and rising from a tie-beam to support a collar purlin. The crown post does not reach ridge level as does the king post.

CRUCK FRAME A frame constructed of large curved timbers extending from ground level to ridge and forming an arch. The frame provides direct support for wall and roof timbers. Cruck-frame members are referred to as blades.

DAMP-PROOF COURSE A layer of impervious material inserted horizontally into a wall to prevent rising damp.

DAUB AND STAVER The Lincolnshire name for wattle and daub.

DEATH-WATCH BEETLE (*Estobium rufoxillosum*) A wood-boring insect which attacks the heartwood of hardwood.

DORMER A window projecting from a pitched roof and having a roof of its own.

DOWN-DRAUGHT A current of air blowing down a chimney flue.

DRAGON BEAM The name given to a large diagonal beam set across a corner to project beyond the angle of a building. The beam is morticed to take jettied floor joists at right angles to each other. The beam is used on buildings with jetty overhangs on two adjacent sides. The beam is supported at the end with a dragon post.

DRAGON POST The post used to support the end of a dragon beam on a building with jetty construction on two adjacent sides.

DRAGON TIE Used at the corner of a hipped roof where the tie takes the foot of the hip.

DRAW BORING When forming a mortice-and-tenon joint, it was common to bore the pin-holes of both members on a slightly different line. As a result, when the timbers were joined and the trenails hammered home, the members were pinched together by tightening of the joint.

DRY-ROT (*Merulius lacrymans*) Probably the most serious of fungi to attack wood in a period timber-framed house.

EAVES The horizontal overhang of a roof as it projects beyond the face of a wall.

EMPRESS A large slate.

ENGLISH BOND In brickwork, an early pattern of alternating courses of headers and stretchers.

EXPANDING BOLT A bolt used to fix timber to masonry when a penetrating bolt cannot be used.

FEATHER-EDGE BOARDING Weather-boarding with a wedge-shaped cross-section.

FILLET A small rectangular member in a moulding.

FINIAL A short post fixed at the end of a ridge and usually joined to the upper ends of barge-boards. Sometimes the finial may be ornamental.

FIRRING PIECES Pieces of timber cut to a long wedge and fixed to the top face of a joist to make a fall in one direction. Used to form a slight fall on a flat roof.

FLASHING Waterproofing around a chimney stack and adjoining roof angles and joints. Also around vertical tile-hanging to avoid water ingress. Flashing materials are commonly lead, Zincan, Nuralite, etc.

FLAUNCHING The sloped concrete base to a chimney-pot to shed surface water.

FLITCH-PLATE A metal plate which can be slotted into a timber beam and batted through horizontally. The flitch-plate forms a web, restrained either side by the timber member it reinforces (see Fig 78, page 158).

FLUE-LINER A fireproof lining for a chimney flue commonly made of asbestos cement, refractory cement, fireclay or stainless steel.

199

FRAMYNPLACE The medieval carpenter's framing yard.

GABLE The vertical termination of a roof (see 'HIP').

GAMBREL ROOF The roof terminates in a small gable at the ridge.

GIRDER A large scantling timber member supporting two sets of joists to reduce the overall span.

GIRDING BEAM, GIRTH, RAIL A horizontal member in a wall at the level of the upper floor. Runs the full length of a bay or the width of the building. It may be divided by an intermediate post.

GRAVEL A bundle of thatching straw.

GROUND SILL The lower horizontal member of a timber-framed wall.

HAMMER BEAM A horizontal bracket roof style, projecting at wall-plate level to carry arched braces and struts and supported by braces. The hammer beam reduces a span and allows shorter timber members. Lateral pressure is also reduced with this detail.

HARDWOOD Wood from a broad-leaved tree which bears its seeds in a seed case.

HEADER In brick walling, a brick laid within the wall so that only its end is visible. Can also be used in stone walling. Often referred to in discussion on infill panels between timber frames.

HEARTWOOD The centre of a tree trunk.

HIP A timber set at the dihedral angle of the sloping termination of a roof. The angle of a roof formed by the intersection of two slopes of a roof above the projecting corner of a building.

HOPPER In surface water drainage, a collector of water from a roof or pipes and leading to a down-pipe.

HOUSE LONG-HORN BEETLE (*Hylotrupes bajulus*) A wood-boring insect which attacks soft-wood. Found commonly in Surrey.

HOUSED OR ENTRANT A description of the shoulder of a tie-beam lap-dovetail joint to avoid the joint opening up.

HYDROSCOPIC SALTS Chemical salts which take up water.

HYPHAE The strands of a fungus.

INGLENOOK An area under a large chimney often containing a bench upon which people could sit.

INTERRUPTED STYLE Common in northern England, the sill beam or plate is interrupted or broken by principal posts.

JACK A device used by thatchers to carry bundles of straw or reed to the roof.

JAMB The vertical edge of a door or window opening.

JETTY The name given to a projection of joist ends so that the upper floor overhangs a lower floor. A continuous jetty is one where the overhang extends to more than one building.

JOISTS The horizontal supporting timbers in timber-floor construction to which the boards are fixed.

JOWL OR ROOFSTOCK The top of a main post enlarged in section. The detail permits the tie-beam, wall plate and post to be connected together. The enlarged head of any post can be referred to as a jowl.

KING POST In roof construction, a vertical post extending to ridge level from a tie-beam. The term was used to describe crown-post construction.

KNEEPIECE A curved or bent timber set part vertical and part inclined. Base crucks in the Weald are technically kneepieces.

LAITHE HOUSE A development of the long-house. The byre or barn is still attached to the house but is not internally connected to it.

LARGE FRAMING The term used to describe large rectangular wall panels.

LATH A thin strip of timber used as a backing for plasterwork (lath and plaster), or a strip of timber upon which roof tiles are hung. Rent, or split, oak is sometimes used.

LEDGED AND BRACED DOOR A simple door of jointed boards and braced horizontally.

LEDGE CLAMP A further member pegged to the inside face of a timber frame and used to support floor joists.

LEDGER A length of hazel used in thatching a roof.

LIGHT The vertical opening of a window framed with mullions.

LIGNIN A chemical constituent of wood.

LINTEL In timber-framed houses, a horizontal beam, often oak, spanning an opening. For example, fireplace lintel.

LISTED BUILDING The name given to a building included in the statutory lists of Buildings of Special Architectural or Historic Interest.

LONG-HOUSE An early house, divided for part-human and part-animal occupation. Usually opposed doors and a through-passage separated the two sections.

LONG STRAW Another name for wheat straw used in thatching.

MATHEMATICAL TILE A tile which has the appearance of brick and which is used as a vertical cladding to period timber-framed buildings.

MECCANO A patented system of building models using metal bars, brackets, plates, nuts and bolts.

MORTICE As in mortice and tenon. A socket

cut into a member to receive the tenon of an adjoining timber (see TENON).

MULLION A vertical member in a window which sub-divides the opening.

MYCELIUM The name given to the spawn of fungi commonly found in buildings.

NIB On a clay tile, the moulded projection which catches onto the tile batten.

NOGGIN PIECE Wood inserts between joists to prevent lateral movement.

NORFOLK REED A reed found in Norfolk and which is the very best thatching material.

OAK FUNGUS (*Phellinus megaloporous*) This wet-rot is often confused for dry-rot. The death-watch beetle can often be found in timber suffering from this fungus.

ORTHOPHENYL PHENAL A fungicide used to treat cellar fungus (*Coniophora cerebella*).

OUTSHUT OR OUTSHOT An extension to a building under a lean-to or cat-slide roof.

PARGETING Exterior plastering of a timber-framed building. This term is also used to describe the mortar lining of a chimney flue.

PARING KNIFE A thatcher's tool.

PENETRATING DAMP Dampness which enters a wall from the side rather than below as in rising damp.

PENTACHLORPHENOL A general-use wood-preservative fluid for the eradication of fungus and wood-boring insect attack.

PIT SAW A saw operated by two men, one standing in a pit and one at ground level. A log was laid over the pit and cut from end to end.

PLANNING PERMISSION The permission usually necessary from a local authority before alterations to or extension of a building. Especially necessary where a period timber-framed house is affected.

PLATE As in roof plate, wall plate, sole plate. A horizontal timber supporting a super-structure.

PLINTH The base of a wall, sometimes slightly projecting and splayed at the top.

POINTING The outside face of a joint between bricks or stone. Can be flush finished or inset to create a surface water drip.

PORE FUNGUS (*Porian vaillantii*) A form of wet-rot which attacks timber in a saturated condition.

PRENTICE BOARD A timber board fixed to the outside face of a wall to throw water away from the structure.

PRINCIPALS (PRINCIPAL RAFTER) Main rafters in a roof. Usually coincide with bay divisions in a period timber frame.

PURLIN A main horizontal timber in a roof supporting the common rafters and itself carried on the principal rafters. A side purlin

supports rafters, a collar purlin supports a collar.

QUARRY TILE A floor tile made from unrefined and baked clay.

QUARTER The name given to a short stud in timber-frame construction.

QUEEN POSTS A pair of upright posts placed equally on a tie-beam or collar-beam and connecting it to the rafters.

QUOIN The external angle of a wall. Derived from the French *coin* (corner).

RAFTER A roof timber supporting the outside roof covering. Usually slopes from the wall plate to the ridge.

RAIL A horizontal framing member used in door or panelling construction.

RAT-TRAP BOND A bond of brickwork where the bricks are laid on edge. Often this bond was used to save bricks when infilling a panel.

REBATE A groove in the edge of a piece of timber.

RED AND DAUB An alternative name for wattle and daub and common in Cheshire.

RED STANDARD Combed wheat reed for thatching.

REGISTER PLATE A horizontal plate set across a chimney-breast to close a substantial part of the opening. A hood may be fixed to the underside and a flue to the top side to stop the chimney smoking into a room.

RENDERING A covering of cement or lime-plaster to the external face of a wall.

REVEAL The side of a wall opening for a door or window.

RHIZOMORPH The root-like strands of a fungus developing for the hyphae.

RIDGE On a roof, the intersection of main roof slopes at the top. The apex of the roof.

RISER The upright board joined to the treads on a staircase.

RIVEN LATHS Cut timber laths fixed to the outside face of oak studs and used as a base for external plastering.

ROOFING FELT (SARKING FELT) Waterproof felt laid under tile battens and outer tiled coverings to prevent water ingress in the roof void.

RUNNER A length of hazel used in thatching.

SAPWOOD The outer layer of wood of a tree trunk. Usually the sapwood represents the last ten years of the tree's life.

SASH A glazed timber window which slides up and down on cords and pulleys.

SCANTLING In traditional building, 'scant-lings' were small timbers, for example, common rafters. The term is also used to describe the dimension of a timber.

SCARF A general name for a range of joints used in period timber-frame construction.

SCREED A mix of sand and cement applied to a concrete floor to give a smooth and level surface. Often about 2in (50mm) thick.

SEDGE A grass-like plant used in thatching.

SERVICE The apartments at the lower end of a medieval hall used for the storage of food and drink. The buttery held drink and the pantry food.

SHAKES Splits or cracks in the surface of the wood following the line of grain.

SHIPS' TIMBERS An expression of the quality of a timber being suitable for shipbuilding, rather like 'marine plywood' today. Not a specific reference to timber gained from scrapped or dismantled ships.

SHUTTERS Timber boards, side hung on hinges, which can be used to close a window opening.

SINGLE-PILE PLAN A house, one-room deep in plan form.

SINGLE-RAFTER ROOF A roof structure without purlins.

SKEW OR DOVETAIL NAILING When nails are driven in at an angle. Especially used in roofing.

SLAKED LIME (*Calcium hydroxide*) Known as hydrated lime and made by wetting calcium oxide (quicklime).

SMOKE BAY A development of the open hearth in a medieval open hall. The upper portion of a central truss was enclosed to channel smoke towards a louvre. Could also occur near an end wall using this as the rear of the smoke bay.

SOFFIT The underside of a horizontal surface.

SOFTWOOD The wood of a coniferous tree.

SOLAR A private withdrawing chamber in a medieval house, above the parlour or in the upper part of a cross-wing. Literally transcribed means 'room above the floor'.

SOLE PLATE OR SILL BEAM The lowest horizontal member into which the posts and studs of the timber frame are tenoned.

SOMER OR WALL PLATE The upper horizontal timber member in a timber-framed wall panel.

SPANDREL The space between the head of a curved arch opening and a rectangular frame.

SPAR OR LIGGER A device made of hazel used to secure thatch.

SPEY A hazel 'hairpin' to secure thatch.

SPERE A short wing of solid walling projecting from one or both sides of a hall, to screen the entrances.

SPERE TRUSS A truss with two speres leaving a wide central opening and giving access from a cross passage into a hall.

SPLIT RING A type of timber connector suitable for certain repairs in members of period timber-framed buildings.

STICKWORK A form of incised pargeting.

STILE The outer vertical framing member of a door.

STIRRUP In floor-joist repair, a system of metal brackets used to support the end of a rotted joist (see Fig 79).

STRETCHED BRICKWORK Bricks laid so that the long side edge is in view.

STRUT Another name for a brace. The strut is usually a straight member.

STUB TENON JOINT In this joint the tenon does not fully penetrate the member into which it is inserted.

STUD An intermediate member in a timber-framed wall panel.

STUD AND MUD An alternative name for wattle-and-daub construction. Used extensively in the north of England.

STYLOBATE A pad stone upon which the timber frame rests. Common in the North and in cruck construction.

SULPHATE OF AMMONIA Used as a component part of fire-preventative treatment for thatched roofs.

TALLOW DIP An early candle made from animal fat.

TEAZLE TENON Another name for a jowl tenon.

TELL-TALE A device used to measure a rate of movement in a building. Commonly a slither of glass adhesed to either side of a wall crack. Movement in the wall will break the glass and indicate a rate of movement.

TENON As in mortice and tenon. The end of a timber member, reduced in width to form a tongue. This is inserted into a mortice to complete a joint.

THACK The medieval word for thatch.

THATCH A roof covering of reed, straw, sedge, heather, etc.

THATCHING SPUD A tool used to separate thatch when repairs are being carried out.

THROAT The narrowing of a chimney flue above an open fire.

TIE-BEAM The horizontal transverse beam in a roof connecting rafter feet at wall-plate level. The tie-beam counteracts roof thrust and creates triangulation in the frame.

TORCHING The name given to the filling in of the underside face of roof tiles or slates with lime and hair mortar. Only found on roofs without boarding or sarking felt.

TRANSOM A horizontal member subdividing a window opening.

TRENAIL A wooden peg used to secure a medieval joint; for example, a mortice-and-tenon joint is pegged together with a trenail.

TRENCHED as in purlins. In a roof truss with

heavy principal rafters. The purlins are normally inset or trenched into the backs of the principal rafters.

TRIMMER A horizontal member used to section off surrounding timber in a roof or suspended floor, for example, around a dormer window opening or a stairwell.

TRI-N-BUTYLTIN OXIDE A chemical fungicide used on cellar fungus (*Coniphora cerebella*).

TRUSS A triangulated roof frame. A framed structure supporting a roof including a pair of principal rafters, a tie-beam, purlins and common rafters supported on them.

TRUSSED RAFTER ROOF A roof without main trusses but with tie-beams at given intervals. Each pair of rafters is connected via a collar and struts may be present between the collar and rafters.

TUMBLING IN The sloping surface of brickwork between a large chimney-breast and a chimney-stack of smaller size.

TWART SAW A two-handled cross-cut saw used by medieval carpenters to cut large framing timbers.

UNDERBUILT In jetty construction, a wall added at a later date beneath the jetty.

VALLEY On a roof, the internal junction of two inclined roof planes.

VERGES A timber board fixed to the verge of a roof, covering the exposed ends of purlins and wall plates. Otherwise called a bargeboard.

WALL PLATE A horizontal timber at the junction of wall and roof frames. The rafter feet sit on the top face of the wall plate.

WATTLE AND DAUB An infill panel in period timber-framed wall construction.

WEALDEN HOUSE A late-medieval and Tudor open-hall house, usually small to medium sized. Often based on the floor plan of a larger house, the name derives from the Weald of Kent and Sussex where good examples can be seen.

WET-ROT A general term for fungi which attack and destroy wet wood.

WIND-BEAM A timber connecting opposing rafters.

WIND BRACE Curved timber members set diagonally between principal rafters and side purlins to increase resistance to wind loadings. The wind brace also restrains a roof structure longitudinally. Can be of a tension or arch type.

WOOD-WOOL A patented insulation material used in wall and roof construction.

YEALM A bundle of reed or straw used in thatching.

YEOMAN A name given to the wealthy farmer of late-medieval and Tudor times. The yeoman may be a tenant farmer holding his land on tenure or he may be a freeholder.

YOKE A short timber member joining rafters or cruck blades together near the ridge. Often supports the ridge.

BIBLIOGRAPHY

Brown, R. J., *The English Country Cottage* (Hale, 1979)

Brunskill, R. W., *Illustrated Handbook of Vernacular Architecture* (Faber, 1978)

Buchanan, T., *Photographing Historic Buildings* (HMSO, 1983)

Cunnington, P., *How Old is Your House?* (Alpha Books, 1980)

—— *Care for Old Houses* (Prism Alpha, 1984)

Fry, Eric C., *Buying a House?* (David & Charles, 1983)

Harrison, J. A. C., *Old Stone Buildings* (David & Charles, 1982)

Hewett, C. A., *English Historic Carpentry* (Phillimore, 1980)

Hinde, Thomas, *The Cottage Book* (Peter Davies, 1979)

Johnson, Alan, *How to Restore and Improve your Victorian House* (David & Charles, 1984)

Lander, Hugh, *House and Cottage Interiors* (Acanthus Books, 1982)

—— *The House Restorer's Guide* (David & Charles, 1986)

Mason, R. T., *Framed Buildings of the World* (Coach Publishing House, 1964)

Melville, I. A., and Gordon, I. A. *The Repair and Maintenance of Houses* (Estates Gazette, 1979)

Peters, J. E. C., *Discovering Traditional Farm Buildings* (Shire Publications, 1981)

Powys, A. R., *Repair of Ancient Buildings* (Dent, 1929; reprinted by The Society for the Protection of Ancient Buildings, 1981)

Richardson, Stanley A., *Protecting Buildings* (David & Charles, 1978)

Ryder, Peter F., *Medieval Buildings of Yorkshire* (Moorland Publishing, 1982)

Taylor, Alan, *The Pocket Book of Home Renovation* (Evans, 1980)

Turner, Stuart, *Buying and Renovating a Cottage* (Patrick Stephens, 1982)

West, Trudy and Dong, Paul, *The Timber-frame House in England* (David & Charles, 1980)

Woodforde, John, *The Truth about Cottages* (Routledge & Kegan Paul, reprinted 1979)

INDEX

205